Erickson

Key Figures in Counselling and Psychotherapy

Series editor: Windy Dryden

The *Key Figures in Counselling and Psychotherapy* series of books provides a concise, accessible introduction to the lives, contributions and influence of the leading innovators whose theoretical and practical work has had a profound impact on counselling and psychotherapy. The series includes comprehensive overviews of:

MILTON H.

Erickson

Jeffrey K. Zeig and W. Michael Munion

SAGE Publications

London • Thousand Oaks • New Delhi

SAGE Publications Ltd
6 Bonhill Street
London EC2A 4PU

SAGE Publications Inc.
2455 Teller Road
Thousand Oaks, California 91320

SAGE Publications India Pvt Ltd
32, M-Block Market
Greater Kailash – I
New Delhi 110 048

British Library Cataloguing in Publication data

A catalogue record for this book is available from the British Library

ISBN 0 8039 7574 0
ISBN 0 8039 7575 9 (pbk)

Library of Congress catalog card number available

Typeset by Mayhew Typesetting, Rhayader, Powys
Printed in Great Britain by Biddles Ltd, Guildford, Surrey

This book is dedicated to our children, Nicole Zeig, and Will and Manda Munion. Erickson had an orientation to the future, and these children are our future.

W.M.M. and J.K.Z.

Contents

Acknowledgements

The authors gratefully acknowledge Lori Weiers, who did the lion's share of our word processing. Her dedication, diligence, experience and attention to detail have immeasurably elevated the quality of this book. We also would like to thank Angi Hughes, who completed the word processing on the initial drafts of the manuscript.

We are most appreciative of Mrs Erickson and the Erickson family, not only for all that they have shared of their personal experiences of Dr Erickson, but for their ongoing efforts and contributions to the Milton H. Erickson Foundation. Their work, along with the commitment and energy of the Erickson Foundation staff, is a resource that is invaluable to the entire psychotherapeutic community.

Finally, we would like to acknowledge collectively Erickson's followers and students. This extensive group of remarkable individuals has advanced Ericksonian work and helped countless patients to profit from Erickson's wisdom.

1

The Life of Milton H. Erickson

And remember always that you're unique. And all that you have to do is let people see that you are.

Milton H. Erickson (Erickson and Lustig, 1975: 6)

When Milton Hyland Erickson, MD died on 25 March 1980, more than 750 people were registered for the First International Congress on Ericksonian Approaches to Hypnosis and Psychotherapy. That five-day meeting took place in December 1980 with more than 2000 attendees from more than 20 countries, making it the largest meeting ever held on the topic of hypnosis. Since then, there have been five more Erickson Congresses, with an aggregate registered attendance over those six meetings of more than 10,000 professionals. Internationally, there are more than 75 Milton Erickson Institutes affiliated with the Milton H. Erickson Foundation in Phoenix, Arizona. More than 100 books have been published about or directly related to Erickson and his work. These figures attest to the following that has grown around the unique approach to psychotherapy that Milton H. Erickson developed, embodied and taught. Many approaches to treatment have been directly influenced by Erickson, including Strategic Therapy; Solution-focused Methods; Neuro-Linguistic Programming; Rossi's Mind/Body work; and the Mental Research Institute approach. Moreover, contributors such as Stephen and Carol Lankton have devised ways to incorporate Ericksonian hypnotherapy into family therapy.

Milton Erickson's influence continues to grow. He added more cases to the literature than any other clinician (O'Hanlon and Hexum, 1990).

A Brief Overview

Milton Hyland Erickson was born on 5 December 1901 to Albert E. and Clara F. Erickson in a humble dirt-floor cabin in the mining town of Aurum, Nevada in the Sierra Nevada Mountains. He was the second of eleven children. Of his 10 siblings, one brother and seven sisters survived birth and infancy. The family moved in 1904 to Lowell, Wisconsin, travelling East in a covered wagon, and bought a farm and eventually owned a condensery milk converter. Through Milton's early life, Albert was a miner, cattle herder and farmer, sometimes travelling back and forth between Nevada and Wisconsin, while Clara operated the farm.

Erickson received his primary education in Lowell and Reeseville, Wisconsin. He suffered from a common type of red–green colour blindness, was 'tone deaf' and unable to recognize or produce basic musical rhythms. He was dyslexic to at least some degree. These problems went undetected and apparently did not prevent him from obtaining an education. By the time he graduated from high school in 1919, he was an accomplished athlete, and had published his first article in a farm journal.

In August 1919, Erickson was stricken with poliomyelitis and was disabled to the degree that he required a year to recover. Erickson's entrance into the University of Wisconsin was delayed until 1920. During his college years he met and married Helen Hutton, with whom he had three children. It also was during this period that Erickson's interest in hypnotic phenomena blossomed. In 1923 he began his first formal course of study into hypnotic phenomena with Clark L. Hull. In 1928, he received both his medical degree and an MA in psychology.

Colorado General Hospital was the site of Erickson's general medical internship, and his psychiatric internship was at Colorado Psychopathic Hospital. In the ensuing 20 years, he held a variety of increasingly prestigious positions. At the State Hospital for Mental Diseases in Howard, Rhode Island (1929) he was Assistant Physician; at Worcester State Hospital in Massachusetts (1930–4) he rose from junior physician to Chief Psychiatrist; at Wayne County General Hospital in Eloise, Michigan he was first Director of Psychiatric Research (1934–9), and later Director of Psychiatric Research and Training (1939–48). Between 1938 and 1948, Erickson rose from instructor to full Professor at Wayne University College of Medicine in Detroit, Michigan. This was also a major transition period in his personal life. In 1935, his marriage of 10 years to Helen ended and he assumed custody of his three children, Albert, Lance and Carol. In 1936, he met and married Elizabeth (Betty) Moore with whom he had five more children, Betty Alice, Allan, Robert, Roxanna and Kristina. Elizabeth Erickson became his fellow researcher, collaborator and life-long companion.

Owing to the extensive research he conducted early in his career, Erickson earned a reputation as a skilled observer. As a result,

Margaret Mead first consulted with him in 1938 to assist in her understanding of spontaneous trance in Balinese dancers. He later collaborated, along with Mead and her husband, Gregory Bateson, in consultation with the US Government's Second World War efforts, by investigating the German and Japanese character structures, and the effects of Nazi propaganda (Rossi *et al.*, 1983).

Erickson moved his family to Phoenix, Arizona in 1948, where he became Clinical Director of Arizona State Hospital for a year. The dry, hot climate provided some relief for his chronic allergies, muscle cramps, intermittent vertigo and other symptoms (probably due to post-polio syndrome, which at that time had not been identified). In spite of the climatic relief to some symptoms, his deteriorating physical condition forced him to resign as Clinical Director and establish a practice out of his home. Here began what Rossi and colleagues (1983) describe as 'the leadership years'.

In the final three decades of his life, drawing upon years of dedicated research and study, Erickson advanced the use of clinical hypnosis through both practice and trainings. He taught his unique style of therapy to thousands of professionals worldwide, wrote or collaborated on scholarly books and papers (over 140 in his lifetime), was a founding member of the Society for Clinical and Experimental Hypnosis (SCEH), and a founder of the American Society of Clinical Hypnosis (ASCH), and its publication *The American Journal of Clinical Hypnosis*. During this period he collaborated and consulted with such luminaries as Aldous Huxley, Andre Weitzenhoffer, Jay Haley, John Weakland, Gregory Bateson and Paul Watzlawick.

When Erickson died, he left behind a loving spouse, four sons, four daughters, sixteen grandsons, sixteen granddaughters. (Now there are 17 of each, and 32 great grandchildren to date.) He also left behind a worldwide following of practitioners influenced directly by his teaching, or indirectly by those who have carried on his work.

The life lived by this man, as described thus far, is impressive by most standards. However, the foregoing has been a deliberately narrow sketch of Erickson and his work – a factual super-structure presented to provide a context against which the nature of the man may be brought out in greater relief. The real essence of Erickson's work and contributions is inextricably intertwined with his character structure, which is evident in how he dealt with the exigencies of his own life. The remainder of this chapter will be dedicated to describing more fully the interplay of Erickson's persona, life experiences, growth and contributions to the field of psychotherapy.

Even prior to his death, some who studied his approach tried to distil theory or technique from their observations of his work, but even the most successful of these efforts fell short. Consider the flight of an eagle documented on film. The beauty and power of the bird is captured; the process of flight is observable, as is its external anatomy. Moreover, the impact of elements such as wind can be inferred. In the end, however, the spontaneity and endless interplay of beast and environment is lost. Similarly, theoretical formulations about Erickson's work do not capture his essence. The results of such efforts are unarguably useful, but they only approximate his approach, which was flexible and characterized by Erickson's ability to mobilize the patient's unique strengths and abilities.

It is this flexibility – this persistent regard for each patient as entirely unique – this attention to all that the patient brings to the therapy situation, that is the foundation for what is perhaps the predominant, guiding principle in Erickson's work: *utilization*. In the simplest of terms, utilization is the readiness to respond constructively to any aspect of the patient's life and experience (Zeig, 1992). Utilization is predicated upon the notion that the most powerful and effective interventions have their origins *within* the patient and his unique circumstances. Utilization, along with five other functional principles that guide the Ericksonian approach, will be discussed in Chapter 2.

Formative Experiences

The origins of Erickson's principle of utilization find parallels even in the moment of his birth. The dirt-floor cabin in which he was born had three walls and relied upon the mountain against which it was built to provide the fourth wall. The family practice was to utilize anything functional at hand in the process of achieving a goal. His mother economically used old whisky bottles for canning jelly (which could be extracted with a knife) in order to reserve the more difficult to obtain wide-mouth jars for solids. Her practice is descriptive of Erickson's approach to treatment; he found economical ways to elicit his patient's resources to resolve a given problem. His therapy was inherently patient-oriented and not disease-oriented. Thus, treatment for two individuals with similar difficulties might vary radically due to their unique personalities and life circumstances.

Erickson approached his work with an overarching sense of curiosity about his patient's unique perceptual point of view. Doubtless, his experience of coping with unidentified perceptual and functional disabilities (dyslexia and colour blindness) underscored for him the uniqueness of any individual's vision of the world.

Parenthetically, it can be noted that Erickson's particular form of colour blindness allowed him to best appreciate purple. As a tribute many of the early books on or about Erickson were printed with a purple jacket cover.

Erickson recounted his experience at age six of finally realizing that there was a difference between a '3' and an 'm.' His teacher guided his hand in writing both a 3 and m. The recognition of difference was not immediate, but a few moments later he experienced what he described as a sudden burst of atomic light. He said the 'm' was 'standing on its legs and the "3" was on its side with the legs sticking out' in the centre of that light (Rossi *et al.*, 1983: 6).

Erickson had a similar experience as a sophomore in high school, when his debate coach found a way, after many other futile efforts, to teach him to say government, as opposed to 'gov-er-ment'. He had been previously unable to even recognize any differences between his mispronunciation and the way others said the word. The teacher inserted the name of one of Erickson's peers, LaVerne, into the word he wrote on a chalk board, spelling it 'govLaVernment'. Once Erickson could pronounce that, she asked him to omit the 'La'. As he read it aloud, he again experienced the blinding flash of light that obliterated everything but the word. He credits that teacher for his method of 'introducing the unexpected and irrelevant into a fixed, rigid pattern to explode it' (Rossi *et al.*, 1983: 8).

These two incidents and others like them made Erickson curious about his own difficulties and how they could be remedied. They also attuned Erickson to the necessity of joining his patients in their perceptual world, rather than doggedly prodding them into 'the real world', as the unsuccessful efforts to get him to write, see or pronounce had done.

A Perceptive Inquisitive Youth

At a young age, Erickson already had a keen eye for noticing what forces maintained a problem, and how he could utilize these forces to resolve it. In recalling what he described as his first use of the double bind, Erickson told of watching his father struggle to lead a recalcitrant year-old calf back into the barn on a blustery winter day. Spurred by young Milton's laughter, Albert challenged him to get the calf into the barn. Erickson responded, after some consideration, by pulling on the calf's tail as his father continued to attempt to lead it into the barn by its head. The calf directed its stubborn resistance at the more annoying of the two forces and dragged Milton into the barn.

Erickson's observational abilities and curiosity melded to form the core of a life-long passion for research. Before the age of 10,

Erickson developed and executed a project to test the validity of his grandfather's method of potato planting, always with the eyes up and during a certain phase of the moon. Erickson planted potatoes with the eyes in various directions and during various phases of the moon, along with a control patch dedicated to grandfather's method. Despite grandfather's disappointing indifference to the result (the test patches produced the same), Erickson had begun a process of developing logical methods for answering his own questions (Rossi *et al.*, 1983). Erickson's curiosity and predilection for seeking out valid answers would later carry his investigations into such diverse domains as hypnotic phenomena, the interplay of criminal tendencies and intellect, schizophrenia and biological changes, experimental neurosis, and, of all things, a transgenerational sneezing phenomena.

At the age of 14, Erickson published his first article, 'Why young people leave the farm', in the *Wisconsin Agriculturist*. The piece was reprinted in the same publication several years later, which is indicative of young Erickson's insight. He would write and publish prolifically for the rest of his life.

Near Death

When 17-year-old Erickson was stricken with polio, he was left with his hearing, his vision and the ability to move his eyes. He had the ability to speak with great difficulty, and few other voluntary physical capabilities. On the day he was stricken, he overheard his mother being told by the doctor that he would die before morning. His outrage at the insensitivity of a mother being told such horrendous news helped fuel his tenacious desire to live. He set the goal of seeing the sun set that night, and requested his mother to rearrange the dresser in a position that allowed him to see into the mirror, through a doorway, and out of a west-facing window. So intent was his desire to see the sunset that he experienced what he later described as an autohypnotic phenomenon: he saw the sunset clearly, but in the process, he mentally blocked out a tree, a fence and a boulder that obstructed his view. Once the sun set, he lapsed into unconsciousness for three days. What followed was a recovery process that required not only tenacity and strength of will, but excellent observational skills and some good fortune as well. Any recovery at all is something of a miracle when one considers that in rural Wisconsin in 1919 there was no modern physical therapy.

A fortuitous event occurred on a day when Erickson was accidentally forgotten, sitting in the centre of the room in a rocking chair contrived to serve as a toilet for the paralysed youth. As he sat there, bored with his immediate surroundings, and wishing profoundly that his chair was sitting next to the window over-looking the farm, the chair began to rock, ever so slightly. Erickson noticed immediately, and came to conclude that his longings were somehow translated into minute muscular impulses. It must have been stunning to learn that his apparently paralysed body was, after all, capable of generating movement! His task then was transformed from achieving the impossible (moving what could not be moved) into expanding upon what is possible (minute movement). It can be noted here that this approach came to characterize much of his later work as a therapist; focusing on positive ability and developing incremental change. Had the potty chair been fashioned from a four-legged base or had Erickson not already possessed an acute observational ability, Erickson's recovery might not have been realized so quickly. It also can be noted that those minute move-ments generated by the unconscious were later understood by Erickson to be examples of ideomotor responses, the way in which unconscious processes affect behavioural change.

Erickson launched a recovery programme based on painstakingly detailed recollections of his specific muscle movements. For example, if the focus was on his hand, then he would recall grasp-ing various items and instances of opening and closing his fingers. He watched the hands and fingers for any twitching or movement, and was spurred on by his successes. He learned that the mere thought of a movement could lead to automatic physical response. During the next 11 months Erickson focused on developing small movements and he learned to expand them in all parts of his body, gradually re-acquiring voluntary control through the experience of memory-induced automatic (ideomotor) movements.

Observation and attention to detail were critical to Erickson's recovery. He was aided in relearning to balance and walk through watching his youngest sister as she moved through the crawling, teetering and walking stages. As his efforts progressed, he learned that exerting himself through walking resulted in fatigue that ultimately reduced his chronic pain. More importantly, he came to discover that he could experience the same pain relief merely by *thinking* about walking, fatigue and relaxation.

Another important outcome of Erickson's early incapacitation was the development of the ability to derive conclusions from information that is customarily disregarded. For example, lying in bed and hearing the barn door shut and foot steps approaching and someone entering the house, Erickson learned to conclude correctly who was approaching and what that person's mood was. This attention to minute details and their implications contributed immensely to his ability as a therapist. When he instructed those who studied with him, he insisted that they attend not only to their patient's gross behaviour and statements, but also to the minutiae of their movements, vocalizations, postures, respiration and so forth.

Expanding Upon Recovery

By the autumn of 1920, Erickson was walking on crutches and ready to enter his freshman year at the University of Wisconsin. At the end of that academic year he was healthier, but still weak and walking with crutches. He was advised by a physician to spend as much time as possible in nature, so he and a friend planned a 10-week canoe trip. At the last minute, his friend decided not to go. Erickson, undaunted, opted to go alone. He left with enough provisions for two weeks, some textbooks and US$4. Along the way he worked for farmers to earn money for food. Sometimes he traded his culinary skills for a share of the meals he cooked for others. Ten weeks later he returned home having canoed 1200 river miles, robust, able to walk with a slight limp, but without crutches and with US$8 in his pocket. Such a journey would be a challenge to a healthy individual, but for someone as physically disabled as Erickson, it represented much more. It symbolized the indomitable will necessary to push his physical endurance in overcoming obstacles such as weather and dams blocking his passage. It symbolized the resourcefulness that located work, food and companionship along the way. It symbolized an implicit philosophy founded on the premise that life presents no challenge without also providing opportunity and a means to over-come that challenge. This tenacity, resourcefulness and positivism are evident not only in the broad scope of work that Erickson pursued during his career, but also in the values he conveyed to patients seeking his guidance.

The Sleeping Journalist

By the time Erickson returned to college for his sophomore year, he understood that the unconscious mind had capabilities that can supplement conscious awareness in dramatic and useful ways. In *Healing in Hypnosis* (Rossi *et al.*, 1983), Erickson told of his first foray into the world of journalism. Recalling that when he was younger, he had corrected arithmetic problems in his dreams, he decided to learn whether he could write editorials for the college newspaper, the *Daily Cardinal*, after he had already gone to sleep. His plan was to study in the evening, go to sleep at 10:30 p.m. set the alarm clock for 1:00 a.m., and when the alarm rang, he would type his editorial, place the typewriter on top of the pages and go back to sleep. The next morning he was surprised to see typewritten pages under his typewriter; he had no recollection of having written anything. He retained the carbon copies without reading them and turned the originals in to his editor. By the end of the week, he had turned in three editorials. Each day he read the newspaper trying to find one of his editorials, but couldn't. At the end of the week, he read the carbon copies of his work and discovered that all three of his editorials had been published, and he had been unable to recognize his own work.

Waking up to Hypnosis

The experience of writing editorials was quite instructive for Erickson. He concluded that 'there was a lot more in my head than I realized' (Rossi *et al.*, 1983: 12). It also gave Erickson a clear sense of dissociative phenomena. He had proved to himself that there was information stored in his mind that was outside of his awareness. At the time, listening to his roommates' description of his behaviour, he concluded that he was walking and typing in his sleep. It was not until his third year in college during Clark Hull's seminar that he began to understand more fully that experience as somnambulistic activity and autohypnosis.

Erickson first encountered hypnosis at age 12 when a friend got a cheap pamphlet on the subject. The friend wanted to hypnotize Erickson, but Erickson declined saying he would wait until he was a man and knew something. Then, he would really learn hypnosis. At the end of his second year of college, he saw Clark Hull demonstrate hypnosis. Erickson convinced one of the subjects to do further work with him. After that, he took what he learned from his first subject and practised on a second, then a third. He spent his spare time the ensuing summer practising hypnosis and devising various techniques to develop subjects' responsiveness. His approach was methodical; he kept notes on his work. He reported on these accomplishments in a seminar he took with Hull and his graduate students during the autumn of his junior year. By the end of that year he hypnotized several hundred subjects and conducted a number of laboratory experiments. He also demonstrated hypnosis at Mendota State Hospital, and to the faculty in the medical school and the psychology departments at the University of Wisconsin.

The seminar with Hull in many ways illustrated Erickson's persona and character. His aggressive experimentation and careful observations during the preceding summer allowed this underclassman to function as a peer among graduate students and one of the leading experts in the field. The participants held widely varying opinions and interpretations of the phenomena and processes involved in hypnosis. Hull's contention was that the 'operator' was far more crucial in eliciting an hypnotic state than any inner processes of the subject. In Hull's conceptualization, the subject was regarded as a passive recipient upon whose blank mind suggestions were imprinted. Hull later developed a standardized hypnotic technique, and ultimately attempted to use induction phonograph records to elicit comparable trance states among different individuals.

In the face of strong opinions by one of the leading experts in the country, Erickson, a 22-year-old undergraduate, held fast to the conceptualizations that his experiences with introspective healing work and his hypnotic experiments with other subjects had given him – that the subject is not a passive automaton, but an active participant. In Hull's conceptualization, hypnosis was done to a subject – in Erickson's, it is elicited in collaboration with a subject. None-the-less, Erickson did profit from the seminars. In addition to the fact that it was an opportunity to hear a wide range of perspectives on hypnotic phenomena, he was exposed to the study of hypnosis through laboratory procedures. He melded what he learned from Hull with teachings on introspection by Tichner, Wundt and Pillsbury to organize his initial laboratory studies of the dynamics of hypnosis and suggestion from the perspective of subject.

The Medical Student

At the age of eight, Erickson made a commitment to become a doctor. Suffering from a severe toothache, he saw the family doctor. He was impressed with this man who not only relieved his pain by pulling the tooth, but gave him a nickel as well. He followed through on his early commitment. As a premedical student, with the recommendation of one of his professors, Erickson worked for the State Board of Control, doing psychological examinations of prisoners and orphans. Later, during medical school, he demonstrated characteristic, but uncommon, resourcefulness. Erickson gave the following account of his first year of medical school to Jay Haley:

> Getting through the first year, when I wanted to be full-time in medical school, there was one serious difficulty – no job. So I went down to the State Board of Control, and beginning in September, every week I had one or two statistical reports on criminality put on the desk of the President of the State Board of Control. They were things he was interested in for getting better appropriations, getting news story releases. Then in November, the first Monday, there was no report. The president was furious, and he demanded that I be called in. He asked me point blank what I was being paid for. Why didn't I have more reports? I told him I wasn't being paid anything. So he said, 'Well, if that's the case you're on the payroll right now!' So that settled my job. In addition to that on every holiday, or vacation, I was paid my expenses and a per

diem for some special examination the State Board wanted. So I was steadily involved. Christmas vacation, if I remember correctly, I was paid 10 dollars a day plus expenses to do examinations. So I managed to make enough money. Also, my first year in medical school I arrived with $75. I bicycled around Madison looking for some opportunity. I saw a house for rent for $70 per month. I looked it over, saw the landlord, gave him $70, and put up a sign, 'Rooms for Students'. I talked the registrar into delaying the payment of fees. I took in students who were working their way through and were delighted to furnish their own linens at a reduced rent. I talked some secondhand storage companies into letting me store some beds and some furniture for them. So I had the place furnished, and the rooms rented out. That essentially paid my way through medical school. Plus I had the regular salary from the Board of Control. I really had a very nice time. (Haley, 1985c: 152–3)

The creative ingenuity illustrated in Erickson's description is characteristic of his approach to life, and became a hallmark of his approach to therapy as well.

As an aside, we can notice how Erickson's character and therapeutic contributions are inextricably intertwined. In contrast, Freud's work stands independently of his persona; one can learn his theories, methods and techniques, and still not have a clear sense of who the man was. Indeed the psychoanalyst is meant to be a shadowy figure to facilitate transference; the analyst's persona is meant to be inscrutable. On the other hand, it is difficult to study Erickson's work without developing a sense of his character. Modelling traits such as perseverance and resourcefulness were part of his therapy.

As it happened, Erickson entered medical school without completing his Bachelor's degree; he delayed completion of his Bachelor's degree because he wanted his thesis to 'be interesting rather than routine' (Haley, 1985c: 153). When he presented his Bachelor's thesis on the interrelationship of feeble-mindedness, abandonment and crime, his committee offered him the option of taking honours on the thesis for his Bachelor's degree, or having it accepted as a combined Master's and Bachelor's thesis, since he was already enrolled in the graduate programme in psychology. So it was that on 18 June 1928 he received both a Master's degree in Psychology and a Medical degree from the University of Wisconsin.

Starting a Family
Three years earlier, in 1925 at 23 years of age, Erickson married Helen Hutton and began a family. He and Helen had three children together; Albert was born in 1929, Lance in 1931 and Carol in 1933. This marriage lasted for 10 years; Milton's divorce from Helen was in 1935. Little is written about how and why that

relationship failed. Rossi and his colleagues (1983), who wrote about this period of Erickson's life, suggests that this painful experience caused Erickson to re-evaluate his perceptions about relationships. He saw gaps in his understanding which he worked to diminish. It was Erickson's general approach to treatment that patients do not necessarily *resolve* life issues definitively; rather, they progress in their development. The task of the therapist is not to solve all present and future difficulties, but to assist the patient past developmental blocks so that they can evolve on their own accord.

Following a medical internship at Colorado General Hospital and concurrent psychiatric internship at Colorado Psychopathic Hospital in 1928–9, Erickson moved to Howard, Rhode Island, where he was appointed Assistant Physician at the State Hospital for Mental Diseases. During his year in this position, he published his first two scholarly papers, focusing on criminal behaviour. Although his interest in hypnosis continued during this period, as was the case in Colorado, the use of clinical hypnosis was formally prohibited. Work and training in hypnosis was limited, therefore, to evenings and weekends.

In 1930, Erickson went to work at Worcester State Hospital in Massachusetts, where he served as Junior Psychiatrist. From 1930 to 1934, he was promoted to Senior Psychiatrist, then Chief Psychiatrist in the Research Service. He published 11 more scientific articles, including 'Possible detrimental effects from experimental hypnosis', the first of his writings about hypnosis (Erickson, 1932). This work reviewed the extant literature, seeking scientific evidence of deleterious effects of hypnosis, such as hyper-suggestibility, alteration of personality, compromise of the subject's ability to distinguish reality from unreality, and development of unhealthy attitudes and escape mechanisms. Nothing in the literature beyond speculation and conjecture could be found to support existent concerns. In Erickson's documented work with more than 300 subjects, in literally thousands of hypnotic sessions, no negative effects were observed.

Along with two other articles on hypnosis, Erickson's writings during this period addressed a variety of issues such as the assessment of delinquents, schizophrenia and its treatment, amnesia and other far-ranging topics. It is clear that young Erickson was interested in all aspects of human functioning and pathology, and articulated his observations and opinions well.

Erickson accepted the position of Director of Psychiatry at Wayne County General Hospital in Eloise, Michigan in 1934. There he researched hypnosis in earnest. His work spanned a wide range of topics including: hypnotically induced neurosis, automatic hand-writing, experiments in sensory perception (including hypnotically induced deafness and hallucinated colour vision), hypnotic treatment of hysterical depression, and the possible anti-social use of hypnosis. He also pursued other areas of research. In all, Erickson published 47 reports during the 14 years he was in Eloise. It is little wonder that these efforts earned him a reputation as a dedicated researcher.

The Research Approach

The quality of Erickson's research made it apparent that he had excellent observational and critical reasoning skills, and that he relied upon research data in formulating his conclusions. The import of his stance is readily illustrated by an analogy from the geopolitical sphere of the 1970s. It is commonly acknowledged that US political relations with communist China could not have been widely accepted internally, unless they were initiated by an ultra-conservative (anti-communist) leader, such as Richard Nixon. Similarly, in the professional climate that historically regarded hypnosis as a first cousin to voodoo and black magic, only reasoned, empirically derived observations could begin to dispel the mysticism surrounding hypnosis, and thus legitimize a powerful therapeutic tool; Milton Erickson's research did just that.

Along with research, Erickson continued to challenge himself to develop his observational abilities. For example, he reported that he would conduct a thorough mental status exam, including delusional and hallucinatory content, avoiding questions about social history, then he would write a detailed speculative social history which he would later compare with the actual history garnered by a social worker. Conversely, he would take a detailed history, then write up a mental status exam, and compare his speculations with the actual exam results. In this way he honed his ability to connect the two types of information and increased his understanding of the relationship between history and ongoing psychiatric symptoms.

The time in Eloise, from 1934 to 1948, was a period of change for Erickson personally, as well as professionally. His marriage to Helen ended in Worcester. It was in Eloise that he met Elizabeth Moore, a student at Wayne University. They married on 18 June 1936. Milton brought to the marriage his children, Albert (7), Lance (5) and Carol (2). Though little is written of the personal experience, Erickson must have been a dedicated father. It was rare in those days for a father to be given custody. In 1938, Betty Alice was born. The family continued to grow with the births of Allan in

1941, Robert in 1945, Roxanna in 1948 and Kristina in 1951. Bert was in his twenties when Kristina was born; as Mrs Erickson said, they had at least one teenager in the family for 30 consecutive years (Haley, 1993).

As he approached 40, Erickson's professional life progressed admirably. In 1939, he was made Director of Psychiatric Research and Training at Wayne County Hospital. That same year he was certified as a psychiatrist by the American Board of Psychiatry and Neurology. Concurrent with his role as Director of Psychiatric Research, beginning in 1934, Erickson joined the faculty at the Wayne University College of Medicine. Beginning as an instructor, he was quickly promoted to Assistant Professor. When he became a certified psychiatrist, he was made Associate Professor (Haley, 1985c). Since he also taught in the Social Services Department, Wayne University made him full Professor in the Graduate School. Michigan State College gave him a professorship in Clinical Psychology, as well. From 1940 to 1955, he was associate editor for the journal, *Diseases of the Nervous System*.

Erickson also volunteered on the local induction board during the war years. This afforded him the opportunity to help the war effort, and at the same time he could take medical and clinical psychology students along so that they would get some practical clinical exposure. In typical Erickson style, he found yet *another* way to benefit from the induction board experience. He wrote about various incidents that happened there, and passed them along to H.C.L. Jackson, a columnist for *The Detroit News*. Jackson published these anecdotes as communications from 'Eric the Badger'. Some of these were even reprinted in the *Reader's Digest*.

In 1938, Erickson was contacted by Margaret Mead, who was studying trance states in Balinese temple dancers, and requested information about hypnosis. She was referred to Erickson by Abraham Maslow. Eventually, Erickson and Mrs Erickson assisted in Mead's project. Together they observed Mead's films of Balinese dancers, many of whom spontaneously developed trance states. There also were dancers who faked trance, and Erickson's task was to discriminate which were genuine. This project initiated a long association between Mead and Erickson.

During the war, Gregory Bateson, along with his wife, Margaret Mead, founded the Center for Intercultural Studies, which provided cross-cultural information to the War Department. At their request, Erickson conducted hypnosis with a Japanese man and had dinner with a German man, during which the man's reactions were observed. Erickson then provided his analysis and observations about cultural differences. Erickson also was an invited speaker and one of the primary subjects of the first Macy Conference in 1952, at which Mead and Bateson were participants. Bateson received an open-ended grant from the Josiah Macy Foundation to pursue any topic he deemed relevant. He assembled a stellar team including Norbert Weiner and eventually, Heinz von Forester. An outcome of the Macy Conferences was the founding of the field of cybernetics. At the first conference, there was no predetermined focus. Erickson's work was studied as a possible departure point.

Although Mead and Bateson divorced in 1950, Erickson maintained a life-long association with both. It was through Bateson's communications research in the mid-1950s that Erickson influenced the development of the strategic and interactional approaches to psychotherapy.

Physical adversity played a major role in Erickson's development. The skills he developed in overcoming the ravages of polio contributed immensely to his understanding of mental processes involved in pain management. Because of polio, he honed his abilities at observing detail and he developed an incredible strength of will.

Again, in Michigan in 1947, physical trauma played a role in the course of Erickson's life and career. A bicycle accident produced a dirt-filled gash in Erickson's forehead. While he knew that he had a sensitivity to horse serum and anti-tetanus toxin, all the best medical advice indicated that risking a reaction to the toxin was the superior option. After a few days deliberation, he took the toxin. A week later he went into anaphylactic shock, which required repeated dosages of adrenaline. Over the next 15 months, he suffered frequent bouts of 'serum sickness' characterized by joint pains, muscle pains and sudden collapse. The long-term effect, however, was the one that most influenced his life – his longstanding allergy to pollen exacerbated dramatically, at times requiring hospitalization. Ultimately, in July 1948, these symptoms led Erickson to travel to Phoenix, Arizona, which, at the time, had relatively few airborne allergens. Following a summer of recuperation, and a conversation with the superintendent of Arizona State Hospital (ASH), Erickson resigned his position at Eloise, and assumed the role of Clinical Director at ASH (Haley, 1985c).

ASH was a programme that had been in a nearly perpetual state of administrative change, owing to contending external political forces. In collaboration with his acquaintance from Detroit, John A. Larson, PhD, MD, Erickson hoped to bring some stability to the programme and to develop it as a progressive research and treatment site. Larson, the superintendent, had a strong research background and had pioneered investigations on the polygraph. The future at ASH looked promising.

As was the case in Eloise, the Erickson family lived in the grounds of the Hospital. Inquiries began to arrive from medical students expressing interest in ASH as a residency site. Two problems disrupted the plans. First, Larson was called away to other duties, which left Erickson with sole responsibility for development of the programme (and for contending with the political processes, as well). Secondly, Erickson suffered recurrent bouts of vertigo, disorientation and disabling pain, which was attributed to residual effects of poliomyelitis and polioencephalitis. These symptoms were too disruptive for the demands of the project. Erickson resigned his position with the Hospital and ventured into private practice.

The House on Cypress Street

Erickson opened his practice in his home for a number of reasons. It afforded easier access to some privacy when self-hypnosis was required to manage the intermittent pain of muscle cramps. Working at home also allowed Mrs Erickson to be available in those instances where the symptoms exacerbated to the point where Erickson required assistance. And, of course, working at home meant more time with his family.

The first home-based practice from 1949 to 1970 was located at 32 West Cypress Street (no longer in existence), in what is now downtown Phoenix. It was in a residential neighbourhood, a short distance from the main street in Phoenix. From 1970 until his death on 25 March 1980, Erickson lived on Hayward Street in another residential area in a home more suited to his disabilities.

Erickson's Cypress Street office was more than unassuming – it was really quite modest. It was a small room in the rear of the house, no more than 10 feet by 10 feet, with three chairs, a desk and a book case. His Hayward Street office was similarly unassuming. Such were the accoutrements of the offices to which 'pilgrims' came from all corners of the earth in search of enlightenment.

Because Erickson's office was in his home, it provided a unique opportunity for 'family' therapy. Erickson's family became involved with the patients. On Cypress Street the family living room doubled as a waiting room. Students, patients and colleagues mingled with children, pets and family friends in a homely way that beautifully reflected Erickson's values – family was prized. More importantly, implicit in integrating patients and family was a positive regard for the patients who came to visit – they were not segregated and isolated. While they waited, they were invited to help dress a dolly, scratch a basset hound behind the ears, or participate in whatever the moment occasioned.

The family shared Erickson's interest in people, and it was not uncommon for one of the girls to make a sandwich for one of the less fortunate patients. One patient who had been hospitalized was 'adopted' by the family after his release. They helped him get a dog which he kept at the Erickson's home (it was not permitted in his apartment house), and which, over the years, he visited and cared for daily (Rossi *et al.*, 1983; Zeig, 1985). It also was common for patients, or even students to do odd jobs around the Erickson home when fees were a problem.

Glimpses of Erickson's family life can be gleaned from the literature since Erickson commonly told anecdotes about interactions with his children to illustrate important points. Also, at some of the International Congresses on Ericksonian Approaches to Hypnosis and Psychotherapy (following his death), the Erickson children have related childhood incidents. One episode concerned one of the boys who insisted that he was old enough to have the responsibility of taking out the garbage. When he failed to follow through on two consecutive days, Erickson intervened. Apologizing profusely, he woke the lad around midnight saying a good parent would have reminded him before bedtime to take out the garbage. Erickson was terribly sorry, but if he wanted to be a good father, he had to be sure that his children followed through with their responsibilities. Would the boy please take out the garbage now, so that Erickson could at least be responsible on the follow through? It seems trash removal was not forgotten after that. Erickson had an iron fist under a velvet glove with both his patients and family.

Lightning Strikes Twice
Starting in 1949 and throughout the early 1950s, Erickson travelled widely conducting workshops and seminars on hypnosis; he also lectured at Phoenix College and Arizona State University. Then, in 1953, Erickson suffered what he believed to be the medical anomaly of a second bout of polio. He thought he had contracted two of the three strains.[1] 'One more to go' he would later quip to Jay Haley (Haley, 1985c: 165). This was characteristic of an attitude that minimized adversity.

The net effect of the 1953 attack was that, thereafter, Erickson was seldom free of pain. There was damage to muscle in his right arm, back, sides, abdomen and both legs. Recovery, however, was facilitated by his prior experience with sense memory exercises; he knew how to retrain damaged muscles to compensate for functional loss. Also, long years of self-hypnosis allowed him to relegate pain management to his unconscious which provided effective relief (Rossi *et al.*, 1983). His level of chronic pain dramatically increased with age. He told of muscle cramps so sudden and severe, that the muscles would literally tear (Haley, 1985c).

Erickson also compensated in mundane ways. He elected not to have a telephone in his Cypress Street office so that he would have to get up and walk to the phone elsewhere in the house many times each day. He engaged in simple tasks, such as peeling potatoes, so that he would retain as much physical function as possible. By 1956 he had regained enough physical strength to climb a mountain with the aid of two canes (Haley, 1985a). In spite of these recuperative gains, there was a persistent, degenerative loss, so that by 1967, Erickson was permanently confined to a wheelchair. By the end of his life, he was in constant chronic pain, breathing by virtue of half a diaphragm and a few intercostal muscles. His vision was double, his hearing was impaired, and he had to relearn to enunciate words clearly because he could no longer wear false teeth. In spite of, or because of, all these adversities, he maintained his good cheer and radiated a joy to be alive that was inspiring and infectious (Zeig, 1985).

Growing Influence

Aside from a period dedicated to initiating the recovery process, the polio did not slow down Erickson's professional development. Indeed, the mid-1950s was a period of growing influence for Erickson. He began to teach hypnosis to psychologists, psychiatrists and dentists at seminars around the country.

During this time, Erickson became friends with Aldous Huxley, and the two collaborated on some intriguing hypnotic work, with Huxley as the subject. The series of experiments was being written up, when a fire destroyed Huxley's Californian home, along with the manuscript and session notes from which it was written. The only documentation of these sessions that remained were some notes that Erickson retained from one of their hypnotic sessions. Erickson wrote and published 'A special inquiry with Aldous Huxley into the nature of and character of various states of consciousness' in *The American Journal of Clinical Hypnosis*, July 1965, which was reprinted in Volume I of the *Collected Papers of Milton H. Erickson on Hypnosis* (Rossi, 1980a).

During their work together, they explored an altered state of mind that Huxley called 'deep reflection', which Huxley commonly utilized in marshalling his resources for writing. The state is characterized by dissociation and amnesia for behaviour and stimuli not central to the chosen focus. Huxley and Erickson also worked with trance states of varying depth while examining variables such as attachment to external reality, the internal sensations of comfort, hallucinations, anaesthesia, amnesia, hypermnesia, time distortion, catalepsy and other common phenomena. In contrasting 'deep reflection' and various trance states, Huxley concluded that while there were some similarities in terms of depth of focus, the hypnotic experience was less related to objective external reality. Despite the loss of the more extensive notes, their written account provides a rich and insightful description of both hypnotic phenomena contrasted with other altered states of consciousness.

Linn Cooper, PhD, approached Erickson regarding his ideas about time distortion and the possibility of using hypnosis as an investigatory tool in manipulating time perception. Erickson was interested as well, and the two collaborated on designing and executing experiments which utilized psychology students at Arizona State University as subjects. While Cooper wrote up the experimental findings, Erickson elaborated on clinical implications and therapeutic applications. *Time Distortion in Hypnosis* was published in 1954. Time distortion was one of the last phenomena of hypnosis to be elucidated. The Cooper/Erickson project was an important contribution to the study of hypnosis.

By the time *Time Distortion in Hypnosis* sold out, and a reprinting was considered, Dr and Mrs Erickson had conducted some exciting experiments that contrasted 'time expansion' with 'time condensation'. These developments called for a second edition (1959) rather than a second printing. This was not the first time that Elizabeth Erickson collaborated with her husband. In fact, they first met when she served as his research assistant in 1935 at Wayne State University. In 1938, they published an article, 'The hypnotic induction of hallucinatory color vision followed by pseudo-negative afterimages' in the *Journal of Experimental Psychology* (22: 581–8). Their work on time distortion was also published in *The American Journal of Clinical Hypnosis* (1958, 1: 83–9).

These joint publications represent instances where the collaboration focused on literary endeavours. However, Mrs Erickson was truly a helpmate in many ways throughout Erickson's career. Occasionally Mrs Erickson would be called in to participate in therapy sessions, for example by demonstrating hypnosis. She assisted, when needed, with his efforts at managing his pain. She worked hard on editing and proofreading *The American Journal of Clinical Hypnosis* during the 10 years Erickson served as its founder and editor. She was hostess to visitors from around the world, and of course, when Erickson was travelling, she shouldered full responsibility in caring for the children. After his death, she continued supporting his work through her duties and as a founding member of the Board of Directors of The Milton H. Erickson Foundation. Her presence and speeches at the Convocations of Congresses, organized by the Foundation, have added an important dimension to the proceedings.

Hypnosis Comes of Age

In 1957, the American Society of Clinical Hypnosis was founded, with Erickson serving two years as its first president. He also began *The American Journal of Clinical Hypnosis*, serving as its first editor from 1958 to 1968. These two events clearly indicated that hypnosis had achieved a legitimacy and acceptance that was unthinkable at the beginning of the twentieth century (hypnosis is discussed in detail in Chapter 3). The acceptance of hypnosis in the professional community was due in no small part to the research-based approach that Erickson took in exploring hypnotic phenomena.

At the close of the 1950s, Erickson was routinely travelling nationally and internationally to present lectures, workshops and seminars on hypnosis. His demonstrations of deep trance phenomena were the centrepiece of these events. The extent of Erickson's expertise with hypnosis is underscored in the demonstration that resulted in the development of the Pantomime Technique.

Erickson gave an invited address in Mexico City to the Grupo de Estudio sobre Hypnosis Clinica y Experimental, which was an affiliate of the American Society of Clinical Hypnosis. Shortly before his address, he was informed that he was to begin his lecture with a demonstration of hypnosis. His subject was a nurse who spoke no English (Erickson spoke no Spanish), had no notion of who Erickson was or anything about hypnosis, and knew only that he was an American doctor who required her silent assistance. She had been assured that she would be treated respectfully. Calling upon some prior experience working with hypnotically induced deafness, Erickson relied upon the nurse's state of mental uncertainty and eagerness to comprehend, to create a readiness to respond to any form of comprehensible non-verbal (pantomime) communication. The induction (and lecture) was a success, and the Pantomime Technique was born. There is no mystery to such an event – Erickson was a master at utilization and had never solely relied on verbal components to elicit trance phenomena.

In 1961, along with Seymour Hershman, MD, and Irving Secter, DDS, Erickson published *The Practical Application of Medical and Dental Hypnosis* (New York: Julian Press). Hershman and Secter also were founding members of The American Society of Clinical Hypnosis. The text was designed for use in the teaching workshops conducted by the society.

By 1960, Erickson had published more than 90 articles and two books, and he was internationally known for his work with hypnosis. The result of this work was that people had begun to seek him out for input and assistance with their own ideas. For example, Jay Haley and John Weakland, working with Gregory Bateson on communications research, approached Erickson in 1955 to learn more about his communication in hypnosis, thinking it was relevant to their understanding of the double bind. They had seen parallels in Erickson's work with patients and communication patterns of 'schizophrenogenic' mothers. Soon, there formed a lasting collaboration between Haley, Weakland and Erickson. These discussions were recorded and eventually transcribed and edited by Haley (1985a, b, c) for publication in the three-volume set *Conversations with Milton H. Erickson, MD*. Much of Haley's work since those meetings was profoundly influenced by Erickson. By the same token, Haley's publication of *Uncommon Therapy* in 1973, profoundly influenced the professional community's collective awareness of Erickson's work. Following *Uncommon Therapy*, interest in Erickson's approach increased dramatically.

Others followed in Haley and Weakland's footsteps. In 1972, Ernest Rossi, PhD, at the instigation of one of his patients, made the trek from Southern California to Phoenix to meet Erickson. This began a relationship that lasted the rest of Erickson's life, and spawned a collaboration on a series of books that consolidated a lot of Erickson's ideas and techniques. Over the years, many experts who learned from Erickson, continue to influence the field of psychotherapy, including Paul Watzlawick, Jeffrey Zeig, Richard Bandler, John Grinder, William O'Hanlon, Stephen Gilligan, and Stephen and Carol Lankton. The extent of his influence on these and other practitioners will be examined in greater detail in Chapter 5.

Hayward Street

When Erickson moved to Hayward Street in 1970, he was mostly retired from practice. To his surprise, a third career developed, that of a teacher. (His first career was as a researcher, second, as a clinician.) Students from around the globe came to Erickson's unassuming home for teaching seminars, beginning in about 1975, to the time Erickson died in 1980. His schedule was full months in advance. One of the seminars is recorded in *A Teaching Seminar with Milton H. Erickson*, edited by Jeffrey Zeig (1980).

The New Mainstream

In spite of his confinement to a wheelchair in 1967, Erickson continued to see patients, collaborate on books and papers, and provide training through the 1970s. His influence on the field of psychotherapy is immeasurable.

Haley (1993: ix) wrote about the change in therapy during the course of Erickson's career – in the 1950s, Erickson's work was unusual, controversial and outside of the mainstream of generally accepted practice, but by the time of his death he was christened as the founder of a major school of therapy, an honour he eschewed, and he *was* mainstream. He had not changed, but the way in which therapy was commonly practised had changed. Family problems might actually be approached by working with the family, rather than with the individual. The problem that brought the patient to treatment could be the focus for treatment rather than being regarded as representative of a deeper underlying pathology. Treatment, within reason, could utilize any approach that resolved the problem. Treatment selection is now most often dictated by the nature of the patient and problem, rather than by methodological bias. And, brief treatment is not only accepted, it is considered to be the desirable choice.

Haley did not suggest that Erickson was responsible for changing the field, although clearly he was influential in those changes. What is probably closer to the truth is that, in the evolution of the practice of psychotherapy, Erickson's predecessors had laid down a solid clinical foundation that clarified thinking about human functioning. Psychodynamic approaches and theory evolved because developmental and unconscious processes influence people; behavioural approaches and theories evolved because people's functioning often is contingent upon learned responses to antecedent stimuli; cognitive approaches address human belief systems; relational approaches address interpersonal functioning. In short, the various schools are descriptive of various *aspects* of human functioning. Erickson eschewed theories in order to see more clearly the essence of his patients, and fit his interventions to their needs. He viewed explicit theories of personality as similar to the mythical Procrustean beds which fit all travellers the same; those who were too short were stretched taller, and those too tall had their legs lopped off to fit the bed.

Erickson serves as a model of treating patients based on their needs and resources. What makes Erickson great is that he brought to this task an incredible understanding of patient's conscious and unconscious resources, and ways in which to mobilize these resources. He was a master at hypnosis, assessment, observation, utilization, and impactful, dramatic communication. These characteristics benefited his patients. However, it was his abilities as a researcher and writer that lent credibility to his work and influenced the field of psychotherapy so dramatically.

Erickson was the recipient of the first Benjamin Franklin Gold Medal by the International Society of Hypnosis in 1977. The same year, *The American Journal of Clinical Hypnosis* published a special issue to commemorate his 75th birthday; Margaret Mead wrote a special tribute for that issue. He was a fellow of eight prestigious professional associations, a Diplomate of the American Board of Neurology and Psychiatry, and an honorary member of seven professional societies internationally in Britain, Japan, Argentina, Spain and Venezuela. He published 147 total books and articles in his lifetime, and the writings about him and his work are innumerable.

On 25 March 1980, Milton Hyland Erickson died. Until shortly before his death, he had been healthy, active and involved in teaching. He was even involved in plans for the first International Congress on Ericksonian Approaches to Hypnosis and Psychotherapy, held in December 1980. In the wake of his death, there were, of course, questions as to whether or not to proceed with the meeting. The organizers apparently made the right choice in proceeding as planned; more than 2000 practitioners attended the first Congress. There have been six more since, and the seventh is scheduled for 1999.

The Milton H. Erickson Foundation in Phoenix, organized in 1979 to continue and advance Erickson's contributions, continues to be a resource to all who are interested in Erickson's work. At the time this book goes to press, there are more than 80 affiliated Erickson Institutes worldwide. The Erickson Foundation also sponsors other annual conferences that bring together exceptional faculty on special topics, such as brief treatment approaches. Every five years, commencing in 1985, the Erickson Foundation has sponsored the Evolution of Psychotherapy Conferences, which feature the acknowledged masters and innovators in the field of psychotherapy who educate, demonstrate, debate and dialogue. These conferences create a unique opportunity for synthesis and growth . . . Erickson would have approved – he was an avid learner and valued integrative approaches to treatment.

Note

1. Again, it is likely that Erickson suffered post-polio syndrome, a malady that was unnamed during his lifetime.

2
Erickson's Primary Contributions

I think anthropology is something all psychotherapists should
read and know about . . . .

Milton H. Erickson (Zeig, 1980: 119)

Erickson's Major Contributions

A 35-year-old married woman came to see Dr Erickson complaining
that she had an airplane phobia and her work required that she fly to
Dallas. She had been a passenger in a plane that safely crash-landed
10 years earlier. During the five years following that crash, she
continued to fly, but experienced mounting fear while the planes
were in the air. Her symptoms ceased as soon as the plane touched
down. The fear was so absorbing that she could not hear, and the
trembling and perspiring became so bad that she had to plan her
business trips to include time for an eight-hour nap and change of
clothes prior to work. She ultimately quit travelling by plane. She
told Erickson that she wanted him to use hypnosis to help her get
over her fear, and that she was a good hypnotic subject. After a trial
of hypnosis, Dr Erickson agreed to help her if she would give a
solemn promise to do *anything* he asked her to do. She consciously
deliberated for five minutes then gave her agreement. Erickson then
required her to go into a trance and give her unconscious agreement,
which she provided more quickly. In trance, she was instructed to
hallucinate flying in a plane at 35,000 feet, and she became fully
symptomatic. She was told, 'And now, I want you to have the plane
descend and by the time it reaches the ground, all your fears and
phobias, anxiety and devils of torture will slide off your body and
into the seat beside you.' She awakened from the trance, glanced at
the empty chair, and ran across the room screaming, 'They are there!
They are there!' When Erickson called his wife into the session and
asked her to sit in that chair, the patient physically restrained Mrs
Erickson from doing so.

At that point, Erickson told the patient that her therapy was
complete, and that she should enjoy her flight to Dallas and back,

and to call him from the airport to tell him how much she enjoyed the flight. He had three photos, varying in exposure, taken of that chair, and sent them to the patient prior to her flight. On the underexposed print he wrote, 'The eternal resting place of your fears, wholly dissipating into space.' The overexposed print was labelled, 'The eternal resting place of your phobias, fears, anxieties and devils of torture slowly descending into the oblivion of eternal gloom', and the properly exposed photo was labelled, 'The eternal resting place of your fears, phobias and anxieties.' She called from the airport, as instructed, and reported that she had an excellent and enjoyable flight. At Erickson's request, she agreed to tell her story to some of Erickson's students.

When she arrived to meet with the students, she avoided the chair and even insisted that none of the students should sit in it. She recounted the experience of her recent flight, after which Erickson had her go into trance and hallucinate a plane ride to San Francisco. There she was to rent a car, drive out to the Golden Gate Bridge, park, walk out to the middle and look down. Erickson kept her there on the centre of the bridge while he told her some history of the bridge, and described the fog rolling in to engulf the bridge. She then awakened from the trance eager to tell of her trip to San Francisco. It was only after recounting her experience that she realized that she had been in trance, and had not travelled to San Francisco.

She was asked to tell the students what other problem she had overcome on her trip to Dallas. She seemed confused, and answered that she didn't have another problem. Erickson told her he would ask a simple question, and she would know what he meant: 'What was the first thing you did in Dallas?' 'Oh, that?' she replied, 'I went to that 40-storey building and rode the elevator from the ground floor clear to the top.' In the past, she had the need to change elevators at each floor because of her fear. Erickson explained to the students that in listening carefully to her symptoms, he had come to understand that she did *not* have a fear of airplanes, as she presented, but had a fear of enclosed places with no visible means of support (planes *in flight*, elevators) as well as a fear of suspension bridges (Zeig, 1980).

Orientation
As the foregoing case study illustrates, Erickson's interventions often were unorthodox, brief and effective. These interventions emanated not from a theory of personality or therapy, but from an orientation toward the patient and the therapy situation.

Chapter 2 provides a historical context for understanding Erickson's work, explains Erickson's refusal to formulate his work into a theoretical system, and expounds upon six practical principles that characterize his orientation toward therapy.

The six principles are:

1. The unconscious mind is an important tool in directing the therapeutic process;
2. Problems are to be regarded as non-pathological, and as a result of people's attempts to adapt to the changing demands of their lives;
3. The therapist may take an active and directive role in the therapy process;
4. Permanent change can and often does emanate from experiences achieved beyond the confines of the therapy room through out-of-session assignments;
5. In most cases the patient possesses adequate resources, strengths, and experiences for the resolution of his or her problems;
6. Effective therapy is predicated upon the utilization of aspects of the patient's problem, life, behaviour and/or functioning.

In Contrast

To understand Erickson's contributions to the field of psychotherapy, it is useful to recall that his early professional development occurred in the 1920s, at a time when Freudian psychoanalytic theory dominated the psychotherapeutic arena, and learning theory (behavioural) and humanistic approaches were in their infancy. Erickson's atheoretical and strategic orientation were a radical departure from mainstream psychotherapeutic thought as then practised. Erickson's practical methods have proven to be a forerunner of the way in which a great deal of therapy is conducted today. Traditional psychoanalytic thought can be conceptualized as a 'physics-based' model because of its method of taking things apart to determine why they work. Erickson's orientation was much more 'anthropological' in that it concerned itself with the 'culture' of the individual, and the special nature of his functioning and adaptations.

In another departure from accepted therapeutic practice, Erickson demonstrated a willingness to focus on the presented symptom rather than looking for 'the root cause' as was the common practice in other therapies. He saw symptoms as attempted adaptations – efforts to cope that were no longer effective. Erickson's contemporaries feared that if the deeper cause of the symptom was not uncovered and resolved, then the patient would simply develop another similar problem (symptom substitution). Erickson believed that by overcoming the problem that brought them to therapy, his patients grew in ways that quite often fostered generative change – a 'snowballing' effect could ensue, generating improvement in overall functioning. The resolution of the original problem might mobilize resources to overcome other problems.

Erickson had studied psychoanalytic theory and achieved a good understanding of it. Some of his earlier writings even had an analytic bent. But in the long haul, he came to believe that the passive psychoanalytic approach which relied upon interpretively derived insights to achieve healing was much too time consuming. None-the-less, Freud's earlier formulation of the unconscious as a major determinant in the functioning of a patient may have influenced Erickson to attend to that mechanism in his efforts to understand and heal his patients. Yet, Erickson did not regard the unconscious as merely a storehouse of recollections to be explored and tapped to achieve restorative insights. He came to regard the unconscious mind as a powerful force that he could utilize in his patient's treatment. He developed new and unique ways to enlist the unconscious in the healing process, often through hypnosis.

Erickson also departed from the humanistic orientation of Carl Rogers. Erickson respected patients and their abilities, strengths and resources necessary for the resolution of their problems. Erickson's approach, however, differed radically from Rogers's client-centred approach. Rogers believed that if the therapist was genuine, accepting and empathic, then all necessary conditions for the healing process were met. Therefore, as long as the therapist remained neutral and allowed the client to lead, healing would occur. In sharp contrast, Erickson was directive. He often had his patients carry out assignments outside of session in environments that were not necessarily characterized by the acceptance and empathy requisite for client-centred therapy.

Atheoretical Approach

Ultimately, Erickson not only declined to align himself with any of the other approaches to psychotherapy that evolved during his career, but hoped that his work would not be codified into a rigid system or school of therapy. He felt strongly that the adoption of any theoretical model narrowly defines and limits the aspects of the patients' functioning upon which the therapist will focus. It also delimits the specific method(s) for instilling change. Erickson eschewed programmed treatment protocols, comparing them to an obstetrician using forceps for every delivery. In an Ericksonian conceptualization, theory-bound practice fails to adequately respect individuals and their intrapersonal assets. He worked to invent a new therapy for each patient, based on that patient's unique situation.

The Ericksonian approach is not stated as a theory of either personality or therapy, but rather emanates from principles which permit the therapist to encounter patients in *their* world. Erickson taught his approaches through demonstration and relating case scenarios to illustrate his points. This style permitted him to teach without uttering dictums (such as 'when working with obsessive compulsives, one should . . .') that might then dogmatically be taken as prescriptive. Instead, his explanations underscored the importance of many factors in therapy: the value of keen observation; willingness to understand the patient's perceptual frame and motivation; an interest in the systemic function of the symptom; creativity in devising interventions that draw upon the patient's strengths and resources; and an acute awareness of communication as the primary agent for creating change. In short, Erickson's 'non-theory' is embedded in his methods and techniques, which are derived from the six principles reviewed in greater detail in the remainder of this chapter.

The Unconscious as a Healing Agent

Erickson respected the unconscious mind – both his patient's and his own. He relied upon both as significant resources in the healing process.

The Therapist

Erickson's experience with the autohypnotic writing of editorials in college convinced him of the creative ability of his unconscious, and he was willing to utilize that source of creativity in his sessions. He related on a number of occasions that he went into an autohypnotic trance during sessions when he believed that he could better understand his patient that way. He recounted writing case notes as he reconstructed a session in which he had been in a trance. He wrote, 'I have amnesia for the interview. I merely pick up my pen and start writing the first note. So, I make a conscious note of that, and I write it down and read it. It's a very delightful experience' (Haley, 1985a).

Erickson also told of doing therapy in trance when he worked with a renowned and rather domineering psychiatrist from another country, who was intellectually sophisticated. Erickson reasoned that the patient was not smarter than Erickson's unconscious, and he approached their first session with the expectation that his unconscious would help to guide the process. Once that first session began, he lost all recollection until he found himself alone two hours later in his office with some therapy notes in a closed folder on his desk. Sessions two through thirteen went the same way. During the fourteenth session the patient suddenly recognized Erickson's state, and shouted, 'Erickson, you are in a trance right now', startling him into a normal waking state, which he maintained for the remainder of their sessions together.

Erickson never examined the notes from the first thirteen sessions, but Ernest Rossi did. Rossi's conclusion was that they were nothing more or less than typical notes a therapist might write (Rossi *et al.*, 1983). We also can conclude that this autohypnotic work must have been satisfactory to this well-schooled patient in order for him to have returned on a regular basis.

Erickson's reliance on his own unconscious was not a form of 'voodoo psychology' in which he turned the session over to 'the all-knowing unconscious' in hopes that somehow the right thing might happen. He spent years consciously developing exceptional observational and communication skills. He had a thorough understanding of psychodynamic theory, psychological functioning and human physiology. In his autohypnotic state he drew upon these vast unconscious resources, but the process was in no way transpersonal. His methods and approaches to psychotherapy were always scientifically and rationally based (E. Erickson, personal communication, 1994).

The Patient

In utilizing his patient's unconscious as a resource, Erickson understood that the unconscious has special forms of processing information. Sometimes work must be conducted in collaboration with the unconscious beyond the awareness of consciousness because the unconscious develops insight in advance of conscious insight.

Often the unconscious speaks symbolically. While it is important to recognize and grasp unconscious symbolism, Erickson pointed out that it wasn't necessary to make implicit meaning explicit. In conversation with Jay Haley (H), Erickson (E) described the following encounter:

> *E*: A patient who came to me launched into a diatribe, vituperative as could be, about her father, and her mother, and her brother. The longer she discussed it the more I realized that she couldn't possibly be talking about her father, her mother and her brother. Then what was it she was talking about?
>
> *H*: You're asking me?
>
> *E*: What was she talking about: father, mother and brother. Her father's god-like dictatorial ways. Her mother's assumption she was the mother of all mankind. Her brother seemed to be a little Jesus. I finally told her, 'I don't quite understand your criticism of your

father, mother, and brother. You seem to be trying to talk about a Trilogy but that's the wrong word. I can't think of the right word.' Trilogy? That's a three: father, mother and brother. Father and his god-like ways, mother the mother of all mankind, brother the little Jesus. Her boyfriend wanted her to become a Catholic, and there was her religious conflicts about the Trinity. She was Protestant, and a very doubtful Protestant. Protestant doubtful, Catholic doubtful. She really wanted that religious question straightened out. She did not want to think that Catholicism had something to do with her doubts about her boyfriend. She just was going to exclude religion from all discussion of her boyfriend. Trilogy? Trinity? And I admitted that trilogy was the wrong word. I couldn't think of the right one.

H: Sounds like your statement about hypnosis. Sometimes you hesitate, seeking for a word so the subject will supply it.

E: That's right. But we got that entire situation straightened out. She just was not going to solve her problem on a religious basis. (Haley, 1985a: 76–7)

In this case the patient alluded to her concerns without being consciously aware that she was talking about religion. Erickson discussed the importance of recognizing when a patient spoke symbolically. The clinician should strive to understand the *real* subject matter, and perhaps address the subject matter, using similar symbolic language.

In another example, the patient unwittingly discussed her feelings about preparing dinner for her husband as a symbol for her attitude toward sex. In this case, Erickson utilized aspects of that process, including setting the table, spicing the meat and establishing the atmosphere in the dining room, in order to address the unspoken problem. In the process, he made it easy for her to be forthright that the real problem was sex. Since the patient did not make the transition to talking about sex, he surmised that her unconscious was prepared to work on the problem, but her conscious was not (Haley, 1985a).

Conscious/Unconscious Split

Erickson elaborated on the difference between the conscious and unconscious processes. He pointed out that the unconscious makes discoveries everyday and consequently guides behaviour. He gave the following example:

In everyday life you show unconscious insight. You step into a social group fully prepared to discuss something, and all of a sudden you discover, 'Well, I'm not going to discuss that. I wonder why.' And you really don't know why. I can think of one of the doctors who's Catholic, and he disagreed with me on the Catholic church in some matters. He presented a case before the staff, and he forgot to mention his recommendation for sterilization. Then after the staff meeting was over, I said,

'You know, Henry, how come you didn't mention sterilization?' Henry said, 'God, that was the entire point of this staff meeting. That's why I presented the patient, to get the staff approval of sterilization. That means I'll have to present it at another staff meeting.' I said, 'Well, why did you forget it?' He said, 'I don't know.' I said, 'Didn't we have visitors?' He said, 'Yes, but what of it?' I said, 'What insignia did those visitors wear?' He said he didn't know. I said, 'You stop and think for a while.' Then he said, 'Oh yes, I just got some kind of a flash that they were wearing something. They were in civilian clothes but they had certain Catholic badges.' Visiting Catholics in a tax-supported hospital? No, you don't mention it. That's unconscious insight. And you see that all the time. (Haley, 1985a: 100)

Importantly, Erickson discussed methods for communicating with the unconscious. There was a young man for whom it was thera-peutic to direct his anger about his father towards his therapist. Erickson found it useful to tell only the patient's unconscious when the next appointment was, thereby facilitating the anger release. He did so by making the occasional random statement about a day or time that was totally unrelated to the subject at hand. This absurdity fostered the anger release and at the same time told the patient's unconscious when to arrive for the next appointment, which the patient did in spite of not knowing how he knew the correct time to show up (Haley, 1985a).

Symptom Focused Non-pathologic Model

While focusing on presenting problems and obvious symptoms, Erickson avoided labelling his patients as sick in terms of being flawed in their personality. A positive approach has a number of benefits. It presupposes a healthy outcome since only symptoms or problems need to be resolved, as opposed to the need for massive personality reconstruction. Implicit in this approach is an appreci-ation for all of the aspects of the individual that are functioning well. This approach also lends itself to brief treatment since the scope is far narrower than pathology based models. Another benefit is that, as a present- and future-oriented treatment, it is more immediately relevant to the patient's current life. Quick results are more appreciable (and thus, encouraging).

An excellent example of Erickson's depathologizing is illustrated in his recounting of his work with a woman who had inhibitions. Briefly, Erickson relieved both Ann's choking spells, which occurred in a variety of situations (predominantly before bedtime) and her unfounded fears. Rather than labelling her as a neurotic (i.e. whole person pathology), when he discussed this case with Haley, Erickson talked instead about, 'That horrible modesty of hers, that horrible rigidity, that horrible punishment of herself . . . She turned her aggressions onto herself. That left her the easy prey of others' (Haley, 1985a: 145–6).

People, Not Problems

There is a distinction between a depathologizing focus on the presenting problems, and focusing myopically on the symptoms without seeing the whole person. Erickson could use diagnostic nomenclature but saw that label as descriptive of the problem, not the person, as illustrated in the following conversation with Jay Haley (H) and John Weakland (W):

> H: Now obviously you don't classify patients the way other people do. A patient comes in the door, and you take a look at the patient and listen to the patient and you don't classify him as an hysteric or as a compulsive . . .
>
> W: Well, you might, but in your operative classification, somehow that isn't the important point, it seems to us.
>
> H: You have some way of classifying people in terms of what they need or what you're going to do, I gather.
>
> E: That is, you recognize the patient as they come in, they may be an hysteric, or a compulsive, or a schizoid or a manic, something of that sort. The problem isn't trying to adapt therapy to that particular classification, but: what potentialities does the patient disclose to you of their capacity to do this or to do that? (Haley, 1985a: 123–4)

Erickson did indeed see the whole person. As a matter of fact, Mary Goulding, who along with her husband Bob Goulding pioneered the development of Redecision Therapy (a synthesis of Gestalt and Transactional Analysis approaches) once commented that 'What people seldom notice or mention about Milton Erickson is that he was a brilliant diagnostician' (M. Goulding, personal communication, Nov. 1994).

Symptoms are Functional

Symptoms can be viewed as simultaneously both problematic and functional. In the case of Ann, cited above, therapy included both improving Ann's functioning in the bedroom, so that the choking was no longer needed to serve her modesty. She could retain the symptom when it was useful – she had attacks during visits from unwelcome guests which ultimately stopped their visits. Erickson recognized not only that symptoms are functional, but that care must be taken while effecting the cure to sometimes leave the symptom at the patient's disposal. He said:

So many therapists, medical men, overlook the patient's rights. They try to relieve a girl of painful menstruation by a blanket removal (e.g. hypnotic anaesthesia). When any girl comes to me to be relieved of painful menstruation I make it very clear to her that she wants to be relieved of the pain of menstruation, as far as she knows. But there certainly is likely to occur, in her lifetime, an occasion in which she might want a painful period. She might like to escape some social engagements, by virtue of complaining about her painful menstruation. She might like to skip the university examination. She might like to get an extra day off from the office. So be realistic about it. She wants to be relieved of painful menstruation when it is convenient for her. The unconscious is a lot more intelligent than the conscious. The girl comes to you for relief of painful menstruation, and you blandly, blithely, give her suggestions to be free, and her unconscious knows that you don't understand the problem. You are telling her now, as a menstruating creature, to be free of pain, and she knows very well that she's going to get married, and she is going to have a baby, and she is going to have interruption of menstruation, and that not one of the suggestions you have given her is so worded that it applies until after she begins a new history of menstruation. She rejects your offering of relief because you haven't taken into consideration the natural course of events. She is acutely aware of that in her unconscious and really scorns you because you just assume that she's never really going to have an interruption. But she is. She may get sick. Maybe in her past she did get sick and had to interrupt menses. And her unconscious, seeking help from you, wants you to consider her as an individual who is going to encounter such and such things. When you give her the privilege of having painful menstruations . . . you have given her the privilege of keeping pain and not keeping it. Then it's her choice, you are not forcibly taking something away from her that she feels belongs to herself. You are just offering her the opportunity of dropping it when it's convenient, and keeping it when it's convenient. (Haley, 1985a: 14–15)

Active Directive Therapist Role

Erickson took a directive role with his patients when indicated, in stark contrast to psychodynamic and client-centred approaches which were prevalent when he began practising. Even cognitive approaches that challenge thinking styles and beliefs, and behavioural approaches that prescribe specific action plans, limit the domains in which the therapist might be directive. But Erickson understood that patients could always accept or reject his advice and, therefore, he was at liberty to provide advice and directive interventions that were quite beneficial to his patients. He recounted:

E: A colleague said he had a minister come to him for psychoanalytic therapy and the minister announced and discussed his plans of visiting a series of bawdy houses. As my colleague thought it over, here's this man with his background and his current occupation. If he goes to bawdy houses, accepts clandestine prostitutes, he may get a venereal disease. If I don't run counter to psychoanalytic theory and practice, and advise the man that there's no hurry about it, no rush about doing it, that he ought not to do it, and really discourage him, I may wreck that man's life. Right then and there my friend decided that he would step in.

Why should I let a girl discuss with me her intention of having an affair without stopping her from it? When I see a man withdrawn from all of his social contacts, even leaving his home town, coming to a strange town to live, withdrawn completely, why should I not select some girl that I know is good company, and safe company, and suggest a luncheon engagement? Why shouldn't I suggest that he join the church choir, instead of letting him fret around in his room wishing hopelessly? Should I let the days and the months and the weeks and the years pass by, while I wait for him? I certainly wouldn't advise a patient to do anything contrary to society. I wouldn't even suggest to a man who's promiscuous that he engage in sexual activity. I would raise the question whether or not he were really interested, and let him examine his urges, see if he's genuinely interested. Phrase the question that he might be more interested in good feminine companionship. (Haley, 1985a: 103–4)

Quicker Pace

Taking a directive role significantly modifies the pace of treatment. In more protracted approaches the therapist requires the patient to develop the prerequisite insight, before behaviour will change. Erickson, on the other hand, routinely found ways for behavioural change to lead, and for insight to follow. Erickson told Jay Haley (H) and John Weakland (W) of a married couple who fought bitterly:

E: For 17 years they've been like that. They've built up a half a million dollar business together. They've got ability. They have worked from 6 in the morning to 10 at night, hard. All they've got is that half a million dollars worth of business. That daily, bitter quarrelling, the nasty things he says about her. She gets even with him. Every Sunday he drives her to the Mormon church. He hates the Mormons. He sits in the car outside the Mormon church waiting for her to get through. For five years they talked to that analyst about – he used to go regularly to the analyst also – about separation, voluntary, legal or divorce.

So I had a joint interview with them. I told him, 'You sit there and you keep your mouth shut.' To the wife, I said, 'And you sit there and you keep your mouth shut. I'm going to summarize this entire thing.' I did it essentially the way I have with you except with much more detail. I said, 'Now you've come to me for therapy, for advice and consultation. It doesn't make a bit of difference to me whether you keep on fighting the rest of your lives or not. It won't make any personal difference to me if you have a voluntary separation or a legal separation or a divorce. You don't have to get any one of them, but if you want any therapy from me, you're going to do one of those three things: voluntary separation, legal separation, or divorce.' They both said, 'This is what we should have been told five years ago.' I said, 'I'll give you an appointment in a week's time. At that time you'll tell me what you're going to do. Then I'll know when I'm going to see you again.' I asked him what he thought of himself, marrying a Mormon girl who had wanted children and, as an engagement present, giving her a vasectomy. I asked her what she thought of herself, giving him as a wedding present a frustrated wife.

W: I think this covers the point I was about to raise because in this case it certainly would seem that, while in some overt respects he was a difficult character, she certainly was going along with it.

E: She matched him kind for kind. He gave her an engagement present of a vasectomy; she countered with that wedding gift, a completely frustrated wife. And 17 years of hammering it home to each other. I'm going to be interested in what they say next Tuesday.

H: What decision they'll make? What do you predict?

E: I ran through the essential details. There are living quarters at their place of business. Now they own a residence right alongside of it. I pointed out that if they had a separation or a divorce, it would have to be genuine. One of them should live at least two miles away from the business. One of them should live in the living quarters of the business, as a watchman, a caretaker during the night. I pointed out to them something they already knew – their business is frequently broken into. They already know that. I thought the man should stay in the living quarters in the business. I thought he ought to go elsewhere and have an apartment. As long as the business was furnishing his living quarters, the business ought to furnish hers. Whenever he needed therapy, he ought to come to me. Whenever she needed therapy, she ought to come to me. Let the business pay for that. And even-steven each take a modest salary from the business.

H: Well, is your goal to get them to separate?

E: Yes.

H: And then to go back on better terms, or a real separation?

E: I told them I thought they ought to separate in an absolutely genuine fashion for six months at least. Maybe they would discover a craving for each other, or they might discover an honestly based hatred. I didn't care which, as long as they really discovered their true feelings. I pointed out to them a voluntary separation is cancelable at any time. A legal separation is cancelable at any time. As for a divorce, you can always remarry. No trouble at all – a two-dollar license fee.

I've urged a couple to go down and get divorced, being perfectly willing to bet that they would remarry, but on a different basis. They didn't know that when they got the divorce. But unless they take some kind of action, they won't discover it. (Haley, 1985b: 149–51)

Sleep or Work

In examining the literature, one can safely conclude that directives, in one form or another, were present in most of Erickson's interventions. Often the directives were simple, but owing to a clear and accurate understanding of his patient, the effects were far reaching.

A man who suffered from insomnia sought help from Erickson. The symptoms began when his wife died. He usually tossed and turned through most of the night, finally falling asleep from 5:00 a.m. to 7:00 a.m. He and his son shared a home and the housework. Erickson learned that the patient detested polishing his hardwood floors, because of the smell of the floor wax. After obtaining a commitment to do as instructed, Erickson told the man he could cure him if he were willing to lose eight hours of sleep. The man said that he had been losing that much every night for the last year, so he agreed. He was instructed to put his pyjamas on and polish his hardwood floor all night long, thus losing only his customary two hours sleep. He was to work all the next day, then polish the floors all night long, repeating the same procedure each consecutive night until he had spent four nights polishing his floors. On the fourth night, the man told his son that he was going to rest his eyes for 15 minutes before he began polishing the floor. He awoke at 7:00 a.m. After that Erickson instructed him to prominently display the can of polish and rag in his home. If he could still read the time 15 minutes after he lay down to sleep, he was to get up and polish the floor all night long. The man was still sleeping regularly one year later. Erickson commented on the case that the patient would do anything to avoid polishing the floor, even sleep (Zeig, 1980).

The intervention in this case, not only varies radically from anything the 'neutral' approaches might do, but it prescribes a behavioural programme that is unlike anything that a traditional behaviourist might design.

Therapy Outside the Session

Taking the Treatment to the Problem
As is implied in the foregoing examples, Erickson recognized that a lot of important therapeutic work could occur outside of the therapy context through the use of task assignments. There are practical reasons for this approach. It has the benefit of engaging the patient in therapeutic work for a greater portion of the week than the allotted session, thus expediting change. It also allows the problem to be confronted in its context of origin, as in the case of insomnia discussed earlier. Tasks also move the nature of the work from the abstract to the concrete. The experience goes well beyond insight or emotional release, it allows for growth that simply cannot be replicated in the therapy room.

Erickson told Gregory Batesen (B) and Jay Haley (H) about Bob who had a very limited number of roads around Phoenix upon which he could drive. Erickson asked Bob:

E: What happens when you try to drive on the street? He said, 'I faint at the wheel.' I asked him if he was sure. He said, 'Yes. My heart starts pounding, and I faint.' I said, 'How do you know?' He said, 'I know. I've had friends with me in the car, and I've tried, and I pass out at the wheel, and they've had to take charge.'

So my approach to him was, 'I'd like to have you go up to Black Canyon Highway and note the telephone poles. Drive up to the last telephone pole that you dare drive up to and stop at the side of it. Then look at the next telephone pole. Drive up there about three in the morning. After you've looked at the next telephone pole, start your car up in forward gear and get it going just fast enough so that when you reach the telephone pole safely, you switch off the ignition. Then you faint as you go past the telephone pole. When you recover, because your car will slow up and you're on the shoulder there', I knew the highway, 'when you recover from the faint, wonder if you can get to the next telephone pole. So put your car into first gear, start it up, release the clutch, and as soon as the engine is really turning, turn off the switch, and see if you get to that third telephone pole before you faint.' You know Bob had just a lot of fun, he got some 20 miles.

B: He got what?

E: He got some 20 miles.

H: How many times did he faint?

E: Oh, a few dozen times, but it got so, towards the last, he was figuring on – can he get another half a mile before he faints? I just had a letter from Bob recently: 'I really enjoyed my vacation trip. I've travelled all through Florida, Alabama, Mississippi, and I'm thinking of staying awhile in Arkansas.' He drove all the way. But you see the willingness to faint was the essential consideration.

H: The willingness to faint.

E: He looked upon the fainting as the absolute barrier to driving. It's not a barrier to driving. You start your car to rolling, you've got the Black Canyon Highway with plenty of room on that shoulder. It's a nice wide highway, you can drive along there on the side of the blacktop. From one telephone pole to the next. Perfectly good. You can start your car rolling, turn off the ignition, and shift into neutral and proceed to faint. Your car is going to come to a stop.

H: You progress by fainting.

E: That's right, and he used each faint as the starting point for the next trip down the highway. You see it was the starting point, not the stopping point. Do you see that? And he travelled down the highway and passed out. (Haley, 1985a: 119)

Assignments outside of the therapy session were commonly used by Erickson. Sometimes they served to develop insight, sometimes they created emotional release, sometimes they broke longstanding behavioural patterns, and sometimes they simply weeded out individuals who were not truly committed to making changes. That last outcome to task assignments, weeding out individuals who are not committed to change, should not be discarded as non-therapeutic. Often confrontation with an assignment forces an individual to see that they choose to continue their problem. Note that this outcome brings the patient to the realization of choice in continuation of the problem, and they may further discover that if they can choose today to continue the problem, then tomorrow they can choose to change.

Other therapies, notably behavioural and cognitive, utilize out-of-session assignments, but these assignments differ vastly from Erickson's work in the degree to which they are individualized, as well as in the array of interventions from which the therapist can select. Cognitive and behavioural tasks are theory driven with some tailoring to the specific patient need, while Erickson's tasks were devised through an interplay of the patient's abilities, strengths, resources and specific problems and needs. Perhaps a contrasting example might be illustrative here. It is not uncommon for individuals suffering from social anxiety who are being treated under the Rational Emotive Behaviour Therapy model (a cognitive/behavioural approach) to be sent to a local shopping centre with instructions to tell a stupid joke to 15 people. The purpose of this 'shame-attacking' exercise would be to challenge their conceptions about their inability to interact socially. The tailoring here might include, for example, considerations about venue options available in the patient's community (e.g. a sporting event versus a shopping centre), or the specific population to be approached (a shy young man might be instructed to approach only females close to his own age). None-the-less, these interventions are 'formula driven' (i.e. a particular class of problem is given a particular class of assignment). Consider in comparison the floor-polishing assignment devised for the insomniac as recounted previously; probably no other individual would have profited from that specific intervention. Creative and uniquely tailored out-of-session assignments were a hallmark of Erickson's approach.

Treatment Draws upon the Abilities and Strengths of the Client

Do What You Can, Then Do What You Can't
Erickson believed that in most cases patients possessed adequate resources, strengths and experiences for the resolution of their

problems. He was keenly aware of how much and what kind of effort his patients could put into their treatment, and he always tailored the interventions to fit their abilities as well as their limitations. A good example of tailoring is to contrast the treatment of another patient with a similar driving problem to that of Bob discussed previously.

E: She lives out beyond Scottsdale, and she couldn't possibly drive on Camelback, which is a few miles north of Cypress Street. She had to go out there by way of McDowell Road. She couldn't go Camelback. These roads are a mile apart. She could go Van Buren. But she couldn't go Camelback, or Indian School, she might possibly go Thomas. She could go McDowell, she could go Van Buren. So, of course, I took in Baseline Road, which would be about five miles out of her way and was south of Van Buren. It would be a ridiculous way of getting to her home. Then I asked her what about this matter of getting absent-minded? 'You know, you drive down Central, and you're headed for McDowell. Why not absent-mindedly turn off of Palm Lane. You can do that. Palm Lane runs parallel with McDowell. Why not cross McDowell in an absent-minded way and go out East Roosevelt, which parallels McDowell? Just do it absent-mindedly. Just be interested in your thoughts.'

H: Hypnosis was involved in this?

E: Usually when I talk to people some hypnosis is involved. [*Laughter*] 'Why not just absent-mindedly drive out East Roosevelt?' That's all I needed. 'Why not plan the next time to go out East Van Buren, and absent-mindedly go out East Roosevelt, which is north of Van Buren? Why not plan to go out Van Buren the next time, and absent-mindedly go out McDowell instead, which is a mile north from Van Buren? Why not absent-mindedly turn left instead of right and go out East Thomas?' I got her to do all those. But remember, I've got her absent-mindedly getting further north and further north, and Indian School is further north. I had her go out East Roosevelt and absent-mindedly turn right on Indian School Road, and she arrived home before she noticed what she was doing.

Well, that settled that. When she told me about that, I pointed out to her very, very emphatically that she had told me that she could not go home by way of Camelback. There was no reason why she should go home, but she was absolutely positive that she couldn't go home by way of Camelback. We repeated that, and repeated that and repeated that. She couldn't go home by Camelback. All I did was drop in one little suggestion; 'Of course you can come in by Camelback.' [*Laughter*] 'But you can't go home by way of Camelback.' You see, you hammer home, 'You can't go home by way of Camelback. You can't, you can't, you can't, you can't. Of course you can come in by Camelback, but you can't go home.' You never forget what you are aiming at. You are aiming at familiarity with Camelback. You emphasize all the can'ts, and you do a thoroughly competent job. Since you agree so wholeheartedly with the patient, they are in a position of yielding that one little inch. They can come in by way of Camelback. That's all you want. One little yielding. (Haley 1985a: 121–2)

Erickson devised this very different intervention utilizing *her* formulation of the problem ('I can't *go home* by way of Camelback Road'), *her* ability to progress 'absent-mindedly', and *her* set of geographic limitations.

Tailoring to the Individual
The individual personality of the patient also is considered in tailoring the style of the approach. Contrast the treatment for Inhibited Ann with that of another couple who had been married for three years. Each was a college professor, and very proper and articulate. In stilted terms, they explained their intense, but unsuccessful, desire to produce children. Each described having 'marital union' twice daily and four times daily on weekends, 'with full physiological concomitants to fulfill our philoprogenitive desires'. They used sesquipedalia and clinical terms as much as possible. Erickson began using polysyllabic speech, much as they did, in order to match their style. They were quite rigid and formal. After listening to their account for some time, Erickson suggested that he believed that they could be cured by shock therapy. He told them there was physical shock therapy and psychological shock therapy, and that they needed psychological shock therapy.

He left them alone to deliberate whether or not they wanted shock therapy. When he returned, they responded that they were prepared. He instructed them that following their shock, they were to remain silent all the way home. He had them each grasp the arms of the chair to prepare for the shock, and said to them, 'You have been engaged in marital union with full physiological concomitants to fulfill your philoprogenitive desires. Now, why in hell don't you fuck for fun, and pray to the devil she isn't knocked up for at least three months. Now please leave' (Rossi *et al.*, 1983: 205). Three months later, the wife was expecting.

Weakland and Haley discuss the contrast of this case, with that of Inhibited Ann.

> W: Well, what strikes me is that with this girl, the main impression I get is that more or less consistently throughout you keep going a step further. You're always going ahead in a somewhat inhibited way. So that these two apparently contradictory things are proceeding sort of together all the time. In contrast, I'm thinking of a couple that you told us about that came to you who were so philoprogenitive that they never enjoyed sex and you listened to them for a half an hour

and all of a sudden said, 'Why don't you fuck for fun?' One seems to me to be a gradual shift, and the other a very abrupt shift.

E: Yes. But, of course, with that couple I told them they needed shock treatment. Well, this girl was shy, timid, fearfully inhibited, and reacting with these choking, gasping attacks upon her own body. This other couple were reacting with more or less paranoid reactions toward each other. 'Getting so I hate him.' 'Getting so I can't stand her.' You see, it's a different type of personality. When somebody says, in the presence of his wife, 'Every time I make love to her now I more or less hate it.' Well, there's a person that can take a hard blow. He's giving a hard blow. When the wife says, in her husband's presence, 'We've tried so hard to get a baby, and it doesn't work, when there's nothing wrong with either of us. And he's just such a disappointment to me.' She's hitting hard too. Now here are a couple of people that can hit hard, but not with malice, with utter earnestness in depicting their situation. If they can hit hard with objective evaluations, so can you hit hard. You're just following their lead.

Here's a woman (Ann) that tucks her skirt in unnecessarily and checks up on it repeatedly, brushes it down. I think you ought to be wary of her sense of modesty. (Haley, 1985a: 138–41)

It is clear that these intervention styles could not be effectively interchanged. Ann got better – losing her dreadful inhibitions. The couple got better, and conceived within months of their single session intervention. Both got better in spite of the fact that the tone and style of intervention varied radically, because Erickson recognized and utilized the individual differences in strengths and limitations.

Individual and Universal Resources

Every person has strengths and resources. Some of these abilities are highly individualized, and some are more universal. For example, only someone who has been musically trained can profit from being reminded how powerful a pianissimo (soft) presentation (in their communication) can be, but nearly everyone has the reference experience of learning to ride a bicycle (a series of failures and successes culminating in mastery) and can draw upon that resource. Erickson utilized both individual and universal reference experiences and resources.

Case Example   There was a woman who was the aunt of one of Erickson's patients living in Milwaukee. She was quite depressed and lived an isolated life. She attended church weekly, but slipped out after the service without speaking to anyone. At the request of the patient, Erickson visited the aunt while he was in Milwaukee to deliver a lecture. He introduced himself making sure she was aware that he was a doctor. He convinced her to give him a tour of her home, and during the tour he noticed her African Violet plants, and one leaf being sprouted to form a new plant. Erickson knew that African Violets require a lot of attention. Before he left, he gave her 'doctor's orders'. She was to buy African Violets, starter pots and gift pots. When there was a christening, a birth, a wedding, an engagement, a sickness or so forth in her church, she was to send a plant. The intervention was a success; by the time of her death she was known affectionately as 'the African Violet Queen of Milwaukee' and her funeral was attended by hundreds. In this excellent example, not only the patient's individual expertise with African Violets was utilized; her community's universal appreciation of a floral tribute was utilized as well (Zeig, 1980).

Utilization

An overarching principle – perhaps THE overarching principle – in Erickson's orientation was that effective treatment utilizes anything that the patient brings to, or that exists in, the therapeutic encounter. Again, utilization is the readiness of the therapist to respond strategically to any and all aspects of the patient or the environment (Zeig, 1992). This, of course, includes both conscious and unconscious offerings, resources, strengths, experiences, abilities (or disabilities!), relationships, attitudes, problems, symptoms, deficits, environment, vocations, hobbies, aversions, emotions . . . the list is endless, but the concept is simple. If it's part of the patient's life, it may be useful in achieving a therapeutic goal AND if the patient brings it, it's probably more potent than anything the therapist can introduce to the situation.

Erickson commented on utilization during a lecture published in *Healing in Hypnosis*:

> You need to think about the manner of feeling, thinking, and emotion the patient has in relationship to the reality of his body and his body experiences at the moment. This morning I was asked a question about the child who comes into the office and races back and forth and is awfully uncooperative. My answer was rather simple. The first thing I would recognize about that child is that his reality is one of racing back and forth; it is one of not cooperating with me. You see that the child is carrying out some motor activity. I think the child had better keep right on carrying out that motor activity because that child needs to work with me. How should the child work with me?
>
> I tell him, 'You are running to this door; you are running up here and you are running toward that door; to this door over here, and back again to that door.' The first thing the child knows he is actually *waiting* for me to tell him which way to run. If the child starts fighting with me [*Erickson gestures to demonstrate a pushing motion*] I may tell him how

now he is pushing with his right hand, then with his left hand. The first
thing you know, the child is waiting for me to say, 'Push me off with
your right hand; now push me off with the left hand!' In other words, the
therapist learns to utilize patients' personal orientations to their situations. You should bear in mind that it's the patients' own mental
processes that allow them to do so. (Rossi *et al.*, 1983: 104)

What the Patient Already has

Sometimes utilization is very simple and concrete. In the case of a
competent industrialist who was hospitalized with depression
secondary to financial ruin, Erickson utilized the man's stereotyped
hand movements to initiate change. The man repetitively moved his
hands in a back and forth manner straight out from his chest, crying
all the while. Erickson told him 'You're a man who has had his ups
and downs', and persuaded him instead to move his hands up and
down. Then, in collaboration with the hospital's occupational
therapist, Erickson put sand paper in the man's hands, and a piece of
wood placed between them, so that he could sand the wood smooth.
Soon the man became interested in the work, and eventually made
wooden chess sets and sold them. The man got well, was discharged,
and in his first year out of the hospital, earned US$10,000 in real
estate, which was a lot of money at the time. In this case, Erickson
utilized the symptomatic compulsive hand movements, made a
'small' variation in direction, and made the symptom productive.
This intervention carried with it the implicit message, '*You are* productive', which the patient carried forth after his discharge (Haley,
1973).

Utilization Outside the Treatment Context

At the end of the first visit to Erickson in 1973 a young Jeffrey Zeig,
who knew of Erickson's appreciation for wood carvings, sought to
express his gratitude for the education he was receiving. He
presented Erickson with a driftwood carving in which only the head
and neck of a duck were finished; the remainder of the piece was
untooled and abstractly resembled a duck's body. Erickson contemplated the art work silently, looking back and forth between
carving and student, and finally uttered the word 'Emerging'. He
utilized the occasion of the gift with it's unique properties, to
communicate a progress report and encouragement to his student.
Erickson wrote,

Therapists wishing to help their patients should never scorn, condemn, or
reject any part of the patient's conduct simply because it is obstructive,
unreasonable, or even irrational. The patient's behavior is part of the
problem brought into the office. It constitutes the personal environment

within which the therapy must take effect. It may constitute the dominant force in the total patient/doctor relationship. So whatever the patient brings into the office is in some way both a part of them and a part of their problem. The patient should be viewed with a sympathetic eye, appraising the totality which confronts the therapist. In so doing, therapists should not limit themselves to an appraisal of what is good and reasonable as offering a possible foundation for therapeutic procedures. Sometimes, in fact, many more times than is realized, therapy can be firmly established on a sound basis only by the utilization of silly, absurd, irrational and contradictory manifestations. One's professional dignity is not involved, but one's professional competence is. (Erickson, 1965a: 57–8)

In a paper originally published in 1959, Erickson told of the application of utilization to an audience member who was the embodiment of resistance:

Another utilization technique was employed during a lecture and demonstration before a medical student body. One of the students proceeded, at the beginning of the lecture, to heckle the writer by denouncing hypnosis as a fraud and the writer as a charlatan, and he declared that any demonstration using his fellow students would be a prearranged hoax perpetrated upon the audience. The measures employed were as follows. Since he persisted in his noisy, adverse comments as the lecture proceeded, it became necessary to take corrective action. Accordingly the lecture was interrupted and the writer engaged in an acrimonious interchange with the heckler, in which the writer's utterances were carefully worded to elicit an emphatic contradiction from the heckler, either verbally or by action.

Thus he was told that he had to remain silent; that he could not speak again; that he did not dare to stand up; that he could not again charge fraud; that he dared not walk over to the aisle or up to the front of the auditorium; that he had to do whatever the writer demanded; that he had to sit down; that he had to return to his original seat; that he was a noisy coward; that he was afraid to look at the volunteer subjects sitting on the platform; that he had to take a seat in the back of the auditorium; that he did not dare to come up on the platform; that he was afraid to shake hands in a friendly fashion with the writer; *that he did not dare to remain silent*; that he was afraid to walk over to one of the chairs on the platform for volunteer subjects; that he was afraid to face the audience and to smile at them; that he dared not look at or listen to the writer; that he could sit in one of the chairs; that he would have to put his hands behind him instead of resting them on his thighs; that he dared not experience hand levitation; that he was afraid to close his eyes; that he had to remain awake; that he was afraid to go into a trance; that he had to hurry off the platform; that he could not remain and go into a trance; that he could not even develop a light trance; that he dared not go into a deep trance, etc.

The student disputed either by word or action every step of the procedure with considerable ease until he was forced into silence. With his dissents then limited to action alone, and caught in his own pattern of contradiction of the writer, it became relatively easy to induce a somnambulistic trance state. He was then employed as the demonstration subject for the lecture most effectively. The next weekend he sought out the writer, gave an account of his extensive personal unhappiness and unpopularity, and requested psychotherapy. In this he progressed with phenomenal rapidity and success. (Erickson, 1959a: 13)

A final example of utilization is illustrated beautifully in an often repeated story about Erickson's then seven-year-old son, Allan. Allan had gashed his leg on a broken bottle while playing outside, and even as he began the process of calming and distracting Allan from his pain, Erickson began to direct Allan's attention toward his longstanding competition with his sister. He got Allan interested in making sure that he didn't get cheated out of getting as many stitches as Betty Alice had gotten previously. The boy not only required no anaesthetic, he repeatedly demanded that the surgeon place the stitches closer together so as to be able to squeeze more in! The surgeon was, of course, astonished, but more importantly, Allan's attention was directed away from the pain of both the cut and the cure. Implicit in his reliance on utilization is Erickson's respectful orientation toward the patient and his or her uniqueness.

Utilization is a concept that is present in virtually all of Erickson's work and in all of the principles described previously in this chapter. It is a cornerstone of the Ericksonian method.

Conclusion

Ericksonian therapy is a radical departure from traditional therapy in many ways. It does not extol insight as critical to outcome; insight may not even occur in successful cases. Erickson was careful not to align himself with any system or theory of therapy on the grounds that adherence to any system of therapy narrows the practitioner's viewpoint and limits treatment alternatives. For that reason, Erickson never formalized his approach as either a theory of personality or therapy.

There are, however, a number of general principles which assist in structuring the therapy process. The astute therapist recognizes that the unconscious not only drives the patient in ways that are often beyond awareness, but it is also a therapeutic ally that is both a source of information and target for intervention. In most cases the patient possesses adequate resources, strengths and experiences for the resolution of his or her problems. It is the task of the diligent professional to identify resources and develop ways to utilize them.

The Ericksonian approach is symptom-based, which facilitates brief treatment. Problems are not viewed as indications of deep-seated pathology, but rather as efforts at adaptation that serve a function. Unfortunately, when these adaptations are unsuccessful or outdated, they present difficulties for the patient. In addressing difficulties, Erickson pioneered methods that broke out of the therapist-as-neutral-observer-interpreter-facilitator mould. He used clinical hypnosis at a time when it had fallen into disfavour. He was directive, offering task assignments and even actively advising against self-destructive behaviour when patients contemplated it. And he moved the domain of therapy beyond the confines of the treatment room with tailored assignments that occurred in the patient's home or community.

This current discourse on theory and principle may provide a useful context in which to view Ericksonian treatment, but the major impact of his work was in the methods and techniques that he advanced. The most prominent of these will be reviewed in detail in the next chapter.

3

Major Technical Orientations

I invent a new theory and a new approach for each individual.

Milton H. Erickson (Lankton and Lankton, 1983: v)

The Art of Therapy

As indicated in the preceding chapter, the major impact of Erickson's work was in the method and techniques he advanced. He is probably best known for the use of hypnosis to precipitate change, which he elevated to an art form. More than anyone else in this century, he is responsible for the widespread use and acceptance of hypnosis. To use a metaphor (another therapeutic technique for which he is well known), if his hypnotic work is an art form, then a trance state is merely the canvas upon which he created, using both bold strokes (positive and negative hallucination, amnesia, age regression and progression, post-hypnotic suggestion, automatic handwriting, direct suggestion) and subtle tones (implication, task assignments, anecdotes, metaphor and paradoxical intervention). Not only was Erickson's palate broad, but he readily borrowed from his patient's palate as well, a method he tabbed utilization.

These 'bold strokes' and 'subtle tones' are, of course, all techniques that Erickson used during trance work. Moreover, he was able to use many of these tools equally effectively without a formal trance induction. As quoted in Chapter 2, he once remarked to Jay Haley, Gregory Bateson and John Weakland that there was probably some hypnosis involved in all of his communication. Thereby, he was alluding to his interaction with the other on the unconscious level, but he was by no means implying formal trance work. Rather, he often conducted hypnotherapy without trance. Some of the techniques he used in formal trance, which also are effective in what he called his 'naturalistic' approach, are metaphor, anecdotes, task assignment, skill building, ambiguous function assignments, implication and paradoxical intervention.

It is useful to remind the reader here that the power of Erickson's work was neither in a theoretical framework nor in the given techniques selected in a particular instance. As asserted in the previous chapter, his interventions were offered in the context of his orientation toward both the patient and problem resolution. In that regard, a complete listing and elaboration of Ericksonian technical contributions here, or anywhere, is impossible. Given full consideration of the uniqueness of each individual, which is penultimate in Ericksonian treatment, and the broad repertoire of therapeutic skills that he brought to the treatment setting, the permutation of possible intervention strategies is quite large. Bearing that in mind, the current chapter examines the techniques listed above with the understanding that the techniques no more constitute Ericksonian therapy than do paints in tubes constitute art.

Hypnosis

Historical Context

In order to understand Erickson's contribution to hypnosis fully, a brief historical overview is provided.

Although there are certainly historical references to phenomena resembling hypnosis that predate Franz Mesmer (1734–1815), it is Mesmer who is most universally considered to be the 'father' of hypnosis (Crasilneck and Hall, 1975). Mesmer posited a theory of animal magnetism, attributing trance phenomena to a transfer of magnetic energy from the hypnotist to patients directly by the Mesmerist, or indirectly through inanimate objects. While he achieved dramatic results, for example, the cure of a case of hysterical blindness, Mesmer fell into disfavour when a special commission of the French Academy of Medicine failed to validate his work. Although he died before the French Academy subsequently issued a favourable report on animal magnetism, the practice of mesmerism was carried forward and extended through the work of individuals like Morton Prince (1854–1929) and John Elliotson (1791–1868).

James Braid (1785–1860) is credited with coining the term 'hypnosis', derived from the Greek word *hypnos* meaning sleep (Crasilneck and Hall, 1975). Braid eschewed the idea of animal magnetism and magnetic theory, and focused instead on the subject's suggestibility. Braid provided an important shift in thinking about the process of hypnosis – conceptually, Mesmerism was done *to* someone, hypnosis was done *with* someone.

Through the second half of the nineteenth century and into the early part of the twentieth century, both the acceptability and theoretical explanation for hypnosis fluctuated. Perhaps the individual who exerted the greatest influence on the use of clinical hypnosis during this period was Sigmund Freud. Initially, Freud was quite interested in the phenomena as a way of accessing and re-experiencing forgotten emotions and events, a cathartic process that produced relief in his patients. However, he became uncomfortable with hypnosis since not all patients responded uniformly to the process. Also, he feared that direct suggestion might remove symptoms that were somehow important for the patient to retain. Freud additionally had concerns over the sexual connotations of the hypnotic process, which can be viewed as the patient 'giving herself' emotionally to the hypnotist. For these reasons, and lacking truly broad experience with hypnosis either clinically or through research, Freud rejected hypnosis. Along with widespread acceptance of his psychodynamic theory and practice, came disrepute for methods rejected by Freud. Thus, growth and exploration within the field of clinical hypnosis were curtailed dramatically until its resurgence, following the First World War, as a method for inducing curative abreaction among traumatized war veterans. By 1923, when Milton Erickson attended Clark Hull's seminar on hypnosis, the negative impact of Freud's earlier rejection of hypnosis had diminished to the point that scholarly individuals had once again begun to examine its nature and applications.

A Difference of Opinion

As stated in Chapter 1, Erickson differed from Hull in that Hull believed that the subject was a passive participant in the hypnotic process. In Hull's conceptualization, a standardized induction would impact each individual in the same way. Deference to Hull's experience, expertise and achievement induced Erickson to refrain from publishing some of his experimental work at that time – Hull's position as one of the founding fathers of experimental psychology in the USA lent credence to his view of the hypnotic process, and may have created some doubt on Erickson's part about relative importance in the roles of operator and subject. The positive upshot of Erickson's experience with Hull was twofold – exposure to Hull and his methods of investigation convinced Erickson that laboratory procedures could be applied to hypnotic phenomena, and the doubt planted by Hull's adamancy probably fuelled Erickson's quest for valid understanding. In the end, of course, Erickson's conclusion was that 'It is what the subjects understand and what the subjects do, not the operators' wishes, that determine what hypnotic phenomena shall be manifested' (Erickson, 1964; Rossi, 1980a: 17).

The Nature of Hypnosis

Once one sheds the notion that the hypnotic experience is a result of some overpowering energy imposed upon the subject by an operator, what emerges is a conceptualization of an hypnotic relationship as an altered state of consciousness produced within, and experienced by, the subject, but influenced to varying degrees by the hypnotist. Erickson offered, 'Hypnosis is the ceasing to use your conscious awareness; in hypnosis you begin to use your unconscious awareness. Because unconsciously you know as much and a lot more than you do consciously' (Zeig, 1980: 39). The trance state is a continuum that is characterized by various states of consciousness. Munion has likened this continuum to a radio band spectrum, with discrete states of consciousness being analogous to particular radio frequencies; one frequency representing, for instance, the state of consciousness experienced when one is absorbed in a good book; one representing that of heated debate; one the creative process; one the dream state; one the hypnotic reality; and so forth. As with radio signals, all frequencies (states of consciousness) available are present (at an unconscious level) at the same time, but the receiver (conscious *awareness*) constantly focuses upon one at a time. Also, communication occurs at both conscious and unconscious levels simultaneously, and as with a radio, the volume (depth of absorption in a given state, i.e. trance depth) can be increased or decreased.

The foregoing metaphor suggests that the hypnotic state is merely one of several naturally occurring states of consciousness, but does little to elaborate or describe what it is. The nature of our being and reality is a result of *what* we think and experience. In that context, our ordinary, non-hypnotic reality is one sort of experience, and hypnotic experience is another powerful and compelling contribution to the totality of our reality.

What is Real?

The nature of the *reality* of the hypnotic experience was articulated quite nicely by a participant in one of Erickson's teaching groups in Phoenix, and reported by Erickson in the 'Further experimental investigation of hypnosis: hypnotic and non-hypnotic realities' (Erickson, 1967). The young woman, in a trance state, had experienced swimming in a lake in Maine, which she reported to the group while still in trance. Through a complex series of tape recordings, she was exposed first in a trance to her description of swimming, then in a waking state with amnesia for her trance experience, to her description of swimming, as well as to her surprised waking reaction to the whole experience.

> She was decidedly startled as she listened to her waking state comments on her first comments on swimming. She listened most attentively, and at the conclusion of the recording she declared.

'I know as an absolute fact that I didn't go swimming in the lake in Maine. That is true, it has to be true. But when I hear my voice telling about it now, I know inside of me that I really did go swimming. The first time when I listened to that other tape recorder, I was just listening to the words and ideas, but when I started listening to the second tape recorder, I heard what I said and I felt my feelings at the same time. Now, to me, in my own feelings, I did not go swimming and I did too go swimming. I know those two thoughts are contradictory when I try to compare them. But when I look at just one set of ideas, I know it is true. Then when I look at the other set, I know equally well that it is true. It's like being in two different worlds of understanding and feeling. But I just want to leave them that way. I don't have any desire or even wish to fit them together. I'm just willing to be in Phoenix and willing to talk to you about being at camp in Maine. But if you put me in a deep trance, I know that I can be anywhere I want to be and the real place where I am won't interfere at all. The way I mean all of that is that I could go swimming in Maine with complete enjoyment and at the same time I could stay in Phoenix and be able to answer all your questions or do anything that you wished without it interfering with the whole experience of swimming. It's like something I often do. I sleep soundly and restfully all night, but I can wake up still tasting that trout I caught in my dream and so happily dressed and cooked and ate with pleasure. But I'm hungry for breakfast in spite of all the trout I dreamed I ate and still taste.' (Erickson in Rossi, 1980a: 78)

The quality of the hypnotic experience – so much more complex, deep and whole than, for example, watching a motion picture – is what makes it *real*. It is that immediacy and reality that makes hypnosis powerful in the therapeutic process. The experience described above is certainly *not* therapy, nor was it intended to be. It was a demonstration of hypnotic process and phenomenology. In considering some of the more common hypnotic phenomena, it is useful once again for the reader to recall that the variety of hypnotic *experience* is virtually infinite since each subject brings his or her own unique history and perspectives to the hypnotic encounter. Erickson was fascinated by hypnotic phenomenology, and dedicated a large portion of his professional work to thoroughly investigating it. He was, in fact, an investigator first, a therapist second and a teacher third.

Common Hypnotic Phenomena

There are a variety of experiences that occur in the hypnotic state which are not a common part of ordinary reality. Here is a partial list of hypnotic phenomena: *amnesia* is a lack of recall which can occur both spontaneously or by suggestion, and can be partial (forgetting a portion of a total experience) selective (specific, forgetting items of an experience), or total; *anaesthesia* is the suppressing of physical sensation, and is most commonly localized; *arm levitation* is the unconscious or automatic lifting of an arm, which is elicited through direct or indirect suggestion; *positive hallucination* involves seeing (or hearing, smelling, etc.) what is not there while *negative hallucination* is to not perceive what is there; *age regression* is experienced as being another, younger age.

These common phenomena are by no means an exhaustive list of the kinds of experiences one can have, but they are illustrative of the variety of unusual possibilities in hypnosis. Erickson used hypnotic phenomena to create therapeutic outcomes.

Anaesthesia
An excellent example of the induction of anaesthesia is provided in this description of hypnotic work with a pregnant woman.

> Now to produce a sacral block in a pregnant woman, I would many times put her in a trance . . . and never mention anything else. I would tell her, 'When you go into the delivery room, think about the sex of the baby, its weight, its appearance and features, whether or not it will have hair. After a while, the obstetrician, who is in full charge of the lower half of your body, will tell you to look and see what your baby is. He will hold it up. [Through that technique] you have a complete sacral block – a total anesthesia.' When my daughter, Betty Alice, had her first baby, the doctor was very worried. He was a student of mine. And she said, 'Don't worry, Doctor, you are an obstetrician, you know your business. In the delivery room you own the lower half of my body, I only own the upper half.' And she started telling the nurses and delivery room personnel about teaching school in Australia. After a while the doctor said, 'Betty Alice, don't you want to know what it is?' And he was holding up a baby boy. She said, 'Oh, it's a boy. Hand it to me. I'm like any other mother, I've got to count its fingers and toes.' She should know what was going on, except she was talking about school teaching in Australia. (Zeig, 1980: 43–4)

The preceding and following accounts were shared by Erickson during a five-day teaching seminar in the summer of 1979 (Zeig, 1980). Erickson recounts another hypnotically induced anaesthesia:

> Now I'll give you another cancer case. A doctor called me and said, 'I have a 35-year-old mother of three children. She wants to die at home. She had a right mastectomy and it's too late. She already has metastases of the bones, her lungs, and more scattered throughout the body. Drugs don't help her one bit. Will you try hypnosis on her?' So I made a house call. As I opened the front door, I heard a chant coming from the bedroom, 'Don't hurt me, don't hurt me, don't hurt me, don't scare me, don't scare me, don't scare me, don't hurt me, don't scare me, don't hurt me.' I listened awhile to that steady chant. I went into the bedroom and tried to introduce myself. The woman was lying on her right side curled

up. I could yell and I could shout and I could repeat myself. And she chanted away constantly.

Then I thought, 'Well, I'd better get her attention some way.' So I joined in her chant, 'I'm going to hurt you, I'm going to hurt you, I'm going to scare you, I'm going to scare you, I'm going to hurt you, I'm going to scare you.' Finally she said, 'Why?' But she didn't wait for my answer, so I continued with my chant only I altered it: 'I want to help you, I want to help you, I want to help you, but I'll scare you, I'll scare you, I'll hurt you, but I want to help you, but I'll scare you, I want to help you.' Suddenly, she interrupted and said, 'How?' and went on with her chants. So I joined in the chant, 'I'm going to help you, I'm going to help you, I'm going to scare you, I'm going to ask you to turn over mentally, just mentally, not physically, turn over mentally, not physically, turn over mentally, not physically, I'll hurt you, I'll scare you. I'll help you if you turn over mentally, not physically.'

Finally, she said 'I've turned over mentally, not physically. Why do you want to scare me?' And then she started her usual chant. So I said, 'I want to help you, I want to help you, I want to help you, I want to help you.' And finally she interrupted herself by saying, 'How?' I said, 'I want you to feel a mosquito bite on the sole of your right foot, biting, biting, it hurts, it itches, it's the worst mosquito bite you've ever had, it itches, it hurts, it's the worst mosquito bite you've ever had.' Finally she said, 'Doctor, I'm sorry – my foot is numb. I can't feel that mosquito bite.' I said, 'That's all right, that's all right. That numbness is creeping up over your ankles, creeping up over your ankles; it's creeping up your leg, over your calf; it's creeping slowly up to your knee. Now it's creeping up your knees and up your thigh, almost halfway, now it is halfway, now it is halfway, now it is all the way up your hips and then it is going to cross over to your left hip and down your left thigh, slowly over your left knee and down, down, down to the sole of your left foot. And now you are numb from your hips down.

'And now that numbness is going to creep up your left side, slowly, slowly to your shoulder, to your neck and then down your arm, all the way to your fingertips. Then it will start creeping up your right side under your arm, and up over your shoulder, and down clear to your fingertips. And now I want the numbness to start creeping up your back, slowly up your back, higher and higher until it reaches the nape of your neck.

'And now we will have the numbness creeping up towards your umbilicus, still higher and I'm awfully sorry, I'm awfully sorry, I'm awfully sorry, but when it reaches the surgical wound where the right breast was, I can't make that numb . . . completely numb. That place where the surgery was done will feel like a very bad itchy, mosquito bite.'

She said, 'That's all right, it's so much better than the way it used to hurt, and I can stand the mosquito bite.' I apologized because I couldn't take away the mosquito bite feeling. But she kept assuring me that she didn't mind that mosquito bite. (Zeig, 1980: 185–7)

Even the reader who is unfamiliar with hypnosis can surmise that Erickson's chanting induction is uncommon. It entails no reference to trance and illustrates beautifully the power of joining the patient at her point of reference. This is an excellent example of how utilization is integrated with hypnosis. Also note that an entry point to 'induction' was the memory of the previous pain of turning over, certainly a novel device.

In another instance:

> A secretary who was a good hypnotic subject called me up on the telephone and said, 'Sometimes when I menstruate I get very severe menstrual cramps. And I am just beginning my menstruation and I've got severe cramps located somewhat to the right side of my lower abdomen. Now, will you give me an anaesthesia for my menstrual cramps?'
>
> I put her into a trance over the phone. I told her, 'You just told me in a waking state about menstrual cramps and you want relief from them. So, understand this, your menstruation will cause you no *further* pain. You will have no more menstrual cramps.' And I emphasized menstrual pain, menstrual cramps. 'Now you wake up.' She awakened, and said, 'Thank you, the pain is all gone.' I said, 'Fine.'
>
> About 20 minutes later she called and said, 'The anaesthesia has worn off. The menstrual cramps are back again.' I said, 'Go into a trance and listen carefully. I want you to develop a hypnotic anaesthesia for menstrual cramps, for menstrual pains of all kinds. Now wake up free of your pain.' She awakened and said, 'This time you gave me a good anaesthesia. Thanks very much.'
>
> A half hour later she called me up and said, 'My menstrual cramps are back again.' I said, 'Your body is a lot wiser than you are. You haven't got menstrual cramps. I gave you a hypnotic anaesthesia, and any doctor knows an acute appendicitis can give you pain like menstrual cramps. I produced anaesthesia for menstrual cramps and I didn't mention your appendix. Call your surgeon.' She did. He put her in the hospital and operated for an acute appendicitis the next morning. (Zeig, 1980: 62–3)

This case illustrates the care that Erickson took, while reaching for a desired outcome, to respect the purpose of the symptom as well as the overt wishes of his patient. Note that unlike the first two cases, Erickson's technique in the third anaesthesia case was quite direct. Again, he did not eschew direct techniques, rather, he knew when to use them.

Contrasting the last two cases illustrates that, in some instances, pain can be entirely eliminated, as (at least briefly) with the secretary, while in others, it is transformed into something less troublesome.

Erickson recognized that pain, like all other symptoms, has a positive function – pain tells us when there is a problem in our bodies, deters us from doing further damage and motivates us to resolve the problem. For example, in the case of the chanting woman, Erickson did not create anaesthesia for her right breast. He surmised she would need some pain as a vent for self-punitive feelings.

Intervention without regard for the positive function of pain would be irresponsible. Notice that Erickson was quite specific in his suggestion, limiting the anaesthesia to the secretary's *menstrual* pain. Anaesthesia, along with arm levitation, was also used for trance ratification.

Arm Levitation

Arm levitation is a phenomenon that was not present in the literature prior to the time when Erickson began his investigations; it is a process that he developed in the course of thousands of hypnotic sessions. Arm levitation is a dissociative process that can occur independently of the conscious will. It differs from anaesthesia in that sensation is not removed in the affected arm. It is related to automatic writing in that it is an active physical response which occurs without conscious direction on the part of the subject.

Rossi (1980a: 1) has pointed out that 'consciousness usually does not recognize when it is in an altered condition'. (He reminds us, by way of analogy, how seldom we realize we are dreaming while we are dreaming.) Erickson utilized arm levitation and other hypnotic phenomena as a 'convincer' to ratify the existence of hypnotic phenomenology for the patient, as well as to gauge the responsiveness of a given subject.

He used direct and indirect methods to elicit arm levitation. Here is a hypothetical example of suggestions that could be interspersed into a flowing induction. 'And it would be *hand*y to recall *right* now, that night *light* you had as a child. And could your memory *float* back to that time . . .'. The italicized words, given special inflection, offer ideas to the unconscious mind to 'hand . . . right . . . light . . . float'. Thereby a sensation of lightness may develop in the right hand which then can begin to rise. The ensuing movement indicates to the hypnotist that the subject is responsive, and when the subject notices his or her hand raised apparently of its own accord, the trance is ratified: consciousness recognizes that it's altered. To play on Rossi's words, in these cases, the dreamer knows he is dreaming, and he is awake to see it for himself. Erickson might also develop arm levitation phenomena differently by inducing catalepsy, a waxy flexibility, whereby he might gently lift the hand and leave it suspended in mid-air. It could remain there apparently with no effort on the part of the subject.

Automatic handwriting (and its variants) is a related and similar phenomenon which allows the unconscious mind to provide information that is unavailable to conscious awareness, through the simple process of placing a pen and paper at the disposal of a hypnotized patient. In working with a woman who had a compulsion to have sex with every and any man she met, Erickson was unable to elicit either an understanding or diminishing of the compulsive behaviour. The patient was a good hypnotic subject, but even automatic handwriting proved fruitless. In a variation on automatic handwriting, Erickson placed a typed manuscript in the patient's hands, along with a pen and instructions to quickly and without conscious consideration 'underline those letters, syllables, words that tell the reason', and she complied. The manuscript was held until the time in which the patient stated she was prepared to learn and understand the reason for her compulsion. Once she read the reason for her behaviour, she realized that in having sex with all men, she was symbolically having sex with her father in an effort to 'make a man of him' and so assist him to overcome his domination by her mother. Her compulsion was cured (Rossi, 1980d: 163–8).

Age Regression

As with arm levitation, Erickson often induced age regression as part of training as a demonstration of trance phenomena. Calling subjects' attention to their past also aids the induction process since it initiates a number of processes sympathetic to the hypnotic process. It directs attention away from the present reality situation and shifts attention from external to internal; it reorients the subject to a time frame that is different with the implication that life was (and, therefore, can be) experienced differently; and this recollection can include school memories (the learning process) thus creating a positive association between the trance experience and new learning.

An example of an age-regression induction with some arm levitation is illustrative.

Case Study   In *A Teaching Seminar with Milton H. Erickson* (Zeig, 1980), the following training experience was recorded. Sally (fictitious name), a female student had arrived late, and Erickson teased and embarrassed her before commencing:

> E: [*Looking to the floor in front of him.*] Now let's lay to rest another firm belief, that in doing psychotherapy you should make your patients feel at ease and comfortable. I have done my best to make her feel ill at ease, conspicuous and embarrassed, and (to the group) that's hardly a way to begin a good therapeutic relationship, is it? [*Erickson looks at Sally, takes hold of her right hand by the wrist and lifts it up slowly.*] Close your eyes. [*She looks at him, smiles, then looks down at her right hand and closes her eyes.*] And keep them closed. [*Erickson takes his fingers off her wrist and leaves her right hand suspended cataleptically.*] Go deeply into a trance. [*Erickson*

has his fingers around her wrist. Her arm drops slightly. Then Erickson slowly pushes her hand down. Erickson speaks slowly and methodically.] And feel very comfortable, very much at ease, and really enjoy feeling very comfortable . . . so comfortable . . . you can forget about everything except that wonderful feeling of comfort.

And after a while it will seem as if your mind leaves your body and floats in space – goes back in time. [*Pause*] It's no longer 1979 or even 1978. And 1975 is in the future [*Erickson leans close to Sally*], and so is 1970 and time is rolling back. Soon it will be 1960 and soon 1955 . . . and then you will know it's 1953 . . . and you will know that you are a little girl. It's nice being a little girl. And maybe you are looking forward to your birthday party or going somewhere – going to visit Grandma . . . or going to go to school . . . Maybe right now you're sitting in the school watching your teacher, or maybe you're playing in the school yard, or maybe it's vacation time. [*Erickson sits back.*] . . . I want you to enjoy being a little girl who someday is going to grow up . . . And the more comfortable you feel, the more like a little girl you feel, because you are a little girl. [*Lilting voice*] Now I don't know where you live, but you might like to go barefoot. You might like to sit in your swimming pool and dangle your feet in the water and wish you could swim. [*Sally smiles a little.*] Would you like your favourite candy to eat right now? [*Sally smiles and nods slowly.*] And here it is and now you feel it in your mouth and enjoy it. [*Erickson touches her hand. Long pause. Erickson sits back.*] Now sometime when you are a big girl, you will tell a lot of strangers about your favourite candy when you were a little girl. And there's lots of things to learn. A great many things to learn. I'm going to show you one of them right now. I'm going to take hold of your hand. [*Erickson lifts her left hand.*] I'm going to lift it up. I'm going to put it on your shoulder. [*Erickson slowly lifts up her hand by the wrist and then puts it on her upper right arm.*] Right there. I want your arm to be paralyzed, so you can't move it. You can't move it until I tell you to move it. Not even when you are a big girl, not even when you are grown up.

Now, first of all, I want you to awaken from the neck up while your body goes sounder and sounder asleep . . . you'll wake up from the neck up. It's hard, but you can do it. [*Pause*] It's a nice feeling to have you body sound asleep, your arm, paralysed. [*Sally smiles and her eyelids flutter.*] And be awake from the neck up . . . And what are some of your memories when you were a little girl? Something you can tell to strangers. [*Erickson leans toward Sally.*]

Sally: [*Clears throat*] I, uh, I remember, uh, a tree and a backyard and umm.

E: Did you climb some of those trees?

Sally: [*Speaking softly*] No, they were small plants. Um, and an alleyway.

E: Where?

Sally: An alleyway between the rows of houses. And all the kids played in the backyard and the back alley.

E: And what did you think, when you were a little girl, you would grow up to be when you are a big girl.

Sally: I thought, um, an astronomer or a writer.

E: Do you think that will happen?

Sally: I think one of them will happen. [*Pause*] I'm – my left hand didn't move. [*Smiles*] I'm real surprised about that. [*She laughs*]

E: You are a little bit surprised about your left hand?

Sally: I recall that you said that it wouldn't move and uh . . .

E: Did you believe me?

Sally: I guess I did. [*Smiles*] I . . . it's very surprising too that you can wake up from the neck up and not the neck down.

E: It's surprising that you what?

Sally: That you can um . . . that your body can be asleep from the neck down and you can be talking – you know and be awake – your body can feel so numb. [*Laughs*]

E: In other words, you can't walk.

Sally: Well, not right this minute. [*Shakes her head.*]

E: Any obstetrician in this group now knows how to produce anaesthesia . . . of the body. [*Erickson looks expectantly toward Sally.*] [*Sally nods her head yes and then shakes her head no. She continues to stare blankly to her right. She clears her throat.*] How does it feel to be 35 years old and unable to walk?

Sally: Uh . . . it feels . . . uh . . . right now it feels pleasant.

E: Very pleasant.

Sally: Uh-hum.

E: Now when you first came in, did you like the joking attitude that I took toward you?

Sally: I probably did.

E: You probably did?

Sally: Yes.

E: Or you probably didn't?

Sally: Yes, it's probably so. [*Sally laughs.*]

E: [*Smiling.*] Now is the moment of truth.

Sally: Well, yeah, I had mixed feelings. [*Laughs.*]

E: You say 'mixed feelings'. Very mixed feelings?

Sally: Well, yeah, I liked it and I didn't.

E: Very, very mixed feelings?

Sally: Uh, I don't know if I can make that distinction.

E: Did you wish to hell you hadn't come?

Sally: Oh, no, I'm very glad that I came. [*Bites her bottom lip.*]

E: And so, in coming here, you've learned how not to walk.

Sally: [*Laughs.*] Yeah, not to move from my neck down. [*Nodding.*]

E: How did that candy taste?

Sally: [*Softly.*] Oh, real good, but . . . uh . . . I had . . . there were several different kinds.

E: [*Smiles.*] Then you have been eating candy.

Sally: Uh-huh. [*Smiles.*]

E: Who gave it to you?

Sally: You did.

E: [*Nods yes.*] Generous of me, wasn't it?

Sally: Yes, it was really nice. [*Smiling.*]

E: Did you enjoy the candy?

Sally: Uh-hum, yes.

E: And all philosophers say, reality is all in the head. (Zeig, 1980: 86–90)

Note that school (with the implication, 'You can learn') is included. The age regression occurs, not to revisit any particular or traumatic event, but to enhance the trance. At the regressed age the subject is induced to hallucinate eating candy and recalls it vividly (this is a gustatory hallucination). She also experiences catalepsy, anaesthesia and paralysis.

To digress briefly, beyond all of those hypnotic phenomena, Sally experienced something else. Erickson's method of initially raising tension by teasing and deliberately making her uncomfortable before he guided her to have an experience that was 'really nice', was seeding a concept he wanted to impress on the students in the seminar. He wanted to underscore that 'pleasant and nice' wasn't an absolute requirement for doing good therapy, and was in some cases a hindrance.

In *The Teaching Seminar*,[1] he went on to tell of treating a girl with anorexia nervosa. Others who had tried to help the girl were 'professional' and reassuring, which fostered mistrust in the patient who didn't believe herself worthy of kind treatment. The others failed. Erickson was firm and heavy-handed with her from the outset, and she perceived him to be genuine since this fitted with the treatment she believed she deserved. She, therefore, followed his instructions and got well. Gentle treatment is not a prerequisite for positive outcome.

February Man

Age regression in a *therapeutic* context is illustrated quite nicely in the case of a woman who was concerned that she might make a poor mother, and was hesitant about becoming pregnant. It seems that throughout her life, her own mother had been quite insensitive to her needs, leaving her care to governesses, boarding schools and summer camps. Affection from mother had been a mere display, lacking in any depth. Father was both more affectionate and more genuine, but also was absent from the home.

Erickson found her to be a responsive hypnotic subject. He regressed her to age five, at which time she came into the family parlour and discovered Erickson waiting there to meet with her father. He introduced himself as the February Man. He engaged her in a conversation during which she displayed a liking for the February Man, who listened attentively to her account of a rather lonesome existence. He told her, he would see her again in June, but saw her sooner. She was regressed to several points during the age of five, allowing the development of a sense of personal and ongoing relationship with the February Man. The regressions continued as fertile encounters at each age through adolescence, with an emphasis on acceptance and providing her with someone to share important life events. The regressed 'visits' were 'timed' to predate or follow important real life events by a few days in order to provide support or to reminisce. The patient had spontaneous amnesia for all of the regressions, and was encouraged in and out of trance not to remember any of the verbal meanings consciously, but to keep and enjoy the emotional values, and eventually share them with her children. Through the course of this treatment the woman displayed an increasing sense of confidence in her ability to parent. She ultimately had three children, which she thoroughly enjoyed (Haley, 1973).

Amnesia

Amnesia can occur spontaneously for part or all of the hypnotic session, or it can be deliberately induced by the hypnotist. If Erickson surmised the conscious mind might be unprepared to accommodate the hypnotic reliving of a repressed traumatic event, then he would suggest amnesia. As discussed in Chapter 2, he might suggest that the unconscious mind filter through unacceptable information gradually, at a pace the patient could handle. Amnesia can be induced indirectly by using distraction. For example, a few remarks about the merits of family vacations and their stress reducing properties might be abruptly inserted into a discourse on the planting and tending of summer squash. The remarks about vacations are likely to be forgotten while the discourse on summer squash may be in itself a point of curiosity. The result of the work might be that a 'workaholic's' family life is improved by taking a summer vacation.

Forgotten Pain

Amnesia proved to be an effective tool in the management of pain for a man in the terminal stages of cancer. In this case, Erickson first helped the gentleman experience relief from a dull throbbing ache through hypnosis that transformed it into a sense of heaviness. The man's experience of pain was modified through both the transformation of the pain, and the *division* of the pain into two kinds – dull/throbbing and sharp/stabbing types of pain. The dull, throbbing pain was successfully transformed into a sense of intense heaviness, after which the brief intense pain was addressed. Time distortion was first introduced so that the periods between sharp pain episodes were perceived as longer, and the duration of the pain was perceived as much briefer. Then amnesia for the pain episodes was induced with the net effect that he no longer looked back on the last episode with distress, or looked forward to the next episodes with dread. The time-distorted (briefer) sharp pain was therefore experienced as a momentary flash that was immediately forgotten. For an individual observing him, the episodes might cause him to pause in mid-sentence, then he would continue on as if nothing happened. The amnesia freed him, not from the sharp pains which continued to reoccur, but from having those pains be the focus of his existence. (Erickson, 1959b; Rossi, 1980c: 258–61).

Practice Makes Perfect

Time distortion and amnesia were again combined to assist a young man who was in danger of losing his job. He was a college student who had a full-time evening job, and a second weekend job playing guitar and singing in a local night club. He had been hired because his music, although unpolished, showed promise. Unfortunately, his demanding schedule allowed him no practice time and he was told that if his playing didn't improve, he would be replaced. This caused him a great deal of anxiety, discouragement and depression, for which he sought treatment from Erickson. Erickson learned that the full-time job was one that was characterized as having both flurries of activity and periods of idleness. The young man proved to be a responsive hypnotic subject and was trained in time distortion, in this case, time expansion. Under hypnosis, he was instructed to use idle times at work to develop brief 10- to 30-second trances during which he was to hallucinate practising his singing and playing. He also was to have amnesia for these trances and for the instructions to have these trances.

The following Monday he reported excitedly that he had performed his best ever on Saturday night. He even compared a tape of his current performance with a tape of a prior performance and confirmed for himself that he was much improved. He was, however, mystified since he had not had time to practise. Under hypnosis, he revealed that each night at work, he averaged at least three long, and several short, practice sessions per shift. During the longer sessions he practised his whole repertoire, and he used the short sessions to review individual songs that needed work. He kept his job *and* got a raise (Cooper and Erickson, 1959).

In both of the foregoing cases, amnesia and time distortion were linked but in different ways. For the dying patient, the experience of duration for something negative was decreased so that it could easily be forgotten, while for the student the experience of time was lengthened so as to allow the student to practise a lot in a short time. Note also that practice was imagined or hallucinated, yet actual performance improved since he kept his job and got a raise.

Hallucination

As noted previously, hallucinations can be either negative or positive. A negative hallucination may be therapeutically useful in removing the perception of something that is inconsequential and that is also problematic. In one case, Erickson worked with an individual suffering from Tourette's Syndrome, which is an uncommon disorder that results in compulsive behaviour, quite often including coarse or vulgar verbalizations. The patient's symptoms first appeared one Sunday morning on the way to church. Upon catching sight of a church building, he found himself uncontrollably uttering obscenities and profanities, grinding his teeth and shaking his fists. Initially, only the sight of church buildings precipitated these episodes, but soon, people dressed in religious garb, discussion of religious matters or religious words, and even a single word of profanity would result in a similar outburst of one to two minutes duration.

The man lost his job as a bartender at an exclusive bar, and ended up working in a tavern where his behaviour was not out of the accepted norm. He became known as 'The Cussing Bartender', and patrons at the bar took it as a challenge to come up with new, obscene phrases that he could not keep from including in his utterances. At one point, his wife swore at him because of the financial problems his undisclosed change in employment was creating, and she experienced in short order what his symptoms were. He had kept this secret from her. She arranged a consultation with Erickson.

The man was agreeable to hypnosis, and proved to be a satisfactory subject. A systematic programme was undertaken to train the man in selective exclusion or alteration of sensory stimuli. Then, utilizing an exhaustive list of stimuli that precipitated outbursts, perception of each stimulus was altered. Thus, churches became 'large, white buildings'; nuns were 'women in silly black dresses'; and religious phrases and profane language became meaningless nonsense syllables. This method also was applied to his self-generated thoughts about religion – they just became strings of nonsense syllables.

Ultimately, he regained his job at the exclusive bar. Over time, he was able to reintegrate words of religious meaning into his vocabulary, and eventually, he was even able to return to church. In this case, a partial negative hallucination was induced in both visual and auditory modalities (Erickson, 1965b).

Crystal Balls

Positive hallucinations can allow individuals to experience as real something they may be unable to imagine or believe. Erickson employed marvellous creativity in using positive hallucinations. An excellent example is the case of a 30-year-old divorced man with a horrible self-concept, a job beneath his abilities, and no friends of either gender. He had few interests, and took all of his meals at the same cheap restaurant. His chief interest was his physical health which he perceived as chronically poor in spite of all medical evidence to the contrary. His doctor sent him to see Erickson, and care was taken to train him in the development of his abilities to experience hypnotic phenomena. Treatment lasted several sessions, and included having him hallucinate a series of crystal balls, in which he could picture the emotional or traumatic experiences of his life. This series of experiences only confirmed for him the hopelessness of his situation. In a waking state he was asked to list his wishes and hopes for himself and his life – the best he could muster for 'dreams' was a mediocre existence of fair health, 'not too much' fear and anxiety, taking all those bad things that would happen 'in stride' and so forth. His hopes in the hypnotic state were similarly dismal. All of his hypnotic work included instruction for amnesia.

Subsequently, the patient was oriented, in a waking state, to the future, when he could look back on the accomplishments of therapy and whatever adjustment he had made in service of creating a more suitable life. This approach allowed him, in trance, to project months into the future and use the skill he already had at viewing the past in crystal balls. In this way he could see his accomplishments as already achieved, which made them much more difficult for him to deny as a possibility. He had amnesia for the future-oriented content of sessions as well. He began making changes in his life – asking for a raise (and receiving a promotion in the process), going out on dates, moving to a better home and so on. One by one he remedied the unnecessary problems in his life, and gave up his preoccupation with being physically ill as well. When Erickson encountered him socially a few years later, he was preparing to marry (Erickson, 1977).

Oral Exams

In yet another interesting case, Erickson induced both negative and positive hallucination, along with several other phenomena. The patient was a physician with a longstanding fear of oral examinations which resulted in psychosomatic symptoms. He had become adept at persuading examiners to give him more strenuous written exams in lieu of an oral exam, and his high level of competence carried him through the increased difficulty. Finally, he was faced with an oral exam for which there would be no exception, and he learned that a man who bore an unreasoning and unexplained hatred for him sat on the examination panel.

When he came to Erickson for help, without asking what treatment would entail, he told Erickson he would do whatever it took to pass that exam. Erickson utilized hypnosis to train the doctor in a variety of hypnotic phenomena, including negative and positive hallucination, amnesia, post-hypnotic suggestion and the ability to appear alert and attentive while in a deep trance. When the man took his oral exam, he was in an undiscernible trance state. He found himself seeing verbal questions as if they were written on a page; he was able to recall information as written in a textbook so that he could read the answer directly, or summarize from the text. At times he experienced the situation as transformed so that it seemed to him he was making rounds with interns and lecturing to them about the questions asked.

In the course of treatment, the patient had a number of positive hallucinations (texts, written questions), and the disappearance of the exam committee was a negative hallucination. Post-hypnotic suggestion, which carries the trance phenomenon forward past the end of the induction, allowed him to experience these sensory alterations outside of the therapy context (Erickson, 1966).

Phenomena vs Techniques
The foregoing portion of this chapter has been, in the main, a discussion and illustration of hypnotic phenomena – events that are *non-ordinary* and constitute the *experiences of the subject*. This is not an exhaustive list of phenomena, but it is adequate to convey a sense of the possibilities of hypnosis. The examples presented illustrated specific hypnotic phenomena, but the reader will note that Erickson often used the same phenomena in different ways. There is a difference between technique and phenomena – phenomena is what can happen, while technique is what is done with the phenomena.

There are a variety of techniques that Erickson either developed, or revolutionized the way in which they were applied. An example of innovative application is post-hypnotic suggestion, a common technique dating back to Mesmer or Braids's period. Then, post-hypnotic suggestion might be as inelegant as 'When you awaken, you will not be afraid.' Contrast this with Erickson's post-hypnotic suggestions for positive and negative hallucinations with the previously described case of the doctor who feared his oral exams.

In the remainder of this chapter, we will examine a number of Erickson's technical innovations. While clarity demands that each technique be discussed separately, the reader should be reminded that Erickson's therapy was never a simple prescription of technique x for problem a. Interventions might include techniques x, y and z, perhaps in the context of deep trance or no trance at all, and with only the individual or with significant other(s) present. Each intervention was tailored to the patient's needs, abilities and resources. In a 75th birthday tribute, Margaret Mead noted that Erickson developed a new technique for each patient (Mead, 1976).

Metaphor

Webster defines metaphor as, 'A figure of speech in which a word or phrase literally denoting one kind of object or idea is used in place of another to suggest a likeness or analogy between them.' It follows, then, that a therapeutic metaphor relates to a patient's particular problem by analogy. The analogy provides information about how to behave more effectively. In Erickson's work, the presentation of the metaphor could be simple or complex, the meaning made explicit or merely implied, and it could be presented in the context of a trance, in conversation or as an activity.

Regardless of the presentation style, metaphor is a powerful intervention for several reasons. First, it engenders little resistance. Since it is only *similar* to the problem, and not the problem, the patient has no investment in holding on to a particular position about the metaphor, as he may have about his problem. Second, the metaphor has the ability to reframe the problem dramatically, much as inserting the name 'LaVern' into Erickson's customary pronunciation of 'gov-er-ment' had done for him as a youth (described in Chapter 1). Third, an effective metaphor often draws upon familiar aspects and ideas in the patient's life, and is therefore personally relevant.

Explicit and Implicit

Erickson (Rossi *et al.*, 1983) told of a woman who had travelled to see him for chronic pain that had been intractable with all prior treatments. During a single two-hour session, he talked to her about hoeing weeds in a garden, and how it is that someone can develop painful blisters, and then develop callouses, so that, over time, they can endure a lot of hoeing without pain. He also discussed how spicy Mexican food may be nearly unbearable to someone who is unaccustomed to it, but the individual who has developed 'callouses' on their taste buds finds the food delightful. He then suggested to her that she could develop callouses on the nerves in the area where she experienced pain. She returned home free of pain. In this case, he clearly (explicitly) connected the metaphors and the problem.

In treating a 10-year-old boy with a bed-wetting problem (Haley, 1973: 199–201), Erickson respected the child's reluctance to discuss his problem. Instead, he entered into a discussion of the boy's enjoyment of playing sports which required strong muscles, co-ordination and timing. From these physical attributes, Erickson moved on to a discussion of muscles and muscle types; flat ones, long and short ones, and finally circular ones that open and close as necessary, like the iris in an eye or the muscle at the bottom of the stomach that holds food back for digestion or lets it go as needed.

In this case the iris and gastric muscles, which already performed with adequate strength, co-ordination and timing, could symbolize the sphincter of the bladder. The boy's bed-wetting abated permanently and the problem was never discussed directly. Here, the metaphor remained implicit.

Simple vs Complex

If the metaphor is appropriate to the problem, a simple metaphor can be astonishingly powerful. A dyed-in-the-wool behaviour therapist sheepishly reported to Munion that in a moment of inspiration (and perhaps desperation) he offered a metaphor (non-behavioural intervention) to a patient with tenacious panic symptoms. 'Your panic is an itch; don't scratch it' he told the patient. To his surprise, as the patient ignored the symptoms, they diminished and disappeared over the next few weeks. Obviously this simple metaphor worked because the patient had a history of success in ignoring an itch. With a similarly simple metaphor, Erickson would occasionally challenge a patient's belief that his problem was impossible to solve. He might present a brain teaser that also seems impossible: How do you plant 10 trees in 5 rows of 4 trees each?[2] Most people struggle with the problem, and conclude that it can't be done. The realization that an unrecognized solution to their problem may exist is inevitable once the solution to the puzzle is revealed. The seemingly unsolvable puzzle is, of course, a metaphor for the patient's seemingly unsolvable problem.

In contrast, metaphors may be long and complex, utilized not only for instructional purpose, but also as a vehicle for engaging attention and deepening a trance state. An example of such a presentation might involve a lengthy story about a gardener carefully tending his young delicate flowers, feeling tired and taking a nap in the sun, having a dream in which a kindly old man inquires about his happiest vision of his life, and being wakened rudely from the dream by a spring rainfall. For this hypothetical patient, the gardening story could be used to induce a light trance state while symbolically underscoring the importance of paying attention to his children. The described dream might be utilized to deepen the trance state and access awareness of life-enriching goals. And waking to the rainfall might help reframe some unpleasant surprises as growth producing. The foregoing illustrative example was contrived for the sake of clarity and brevity; many examples of actual case presentations are available in the literature (see bibliography) but would be too lengthy to reprint here. Lankton and Lankton (1983) cogently describe the process of multiple embedded metaphor in great detail in *The Answer Within*.

Activity

Examples described thus far have involved conversations and inductions, but it is possible for a metaphor to be behavioural as well. In one instance, Erickson (Rosen, 1982: 176–7) was treating a construction worker who had fallen 40 storeys and suffered chronic pain. The man was also unable to continue practising his trade, which had been a source of positive self-esteem and gratification. In addition to utilizing a verbal metaphor for pain reduction, Erickson also devised a behavioural metaphor that attended to the patient's lost ability to work for a living. He had the man compile scrapbooks full of humorous cartoons, jokes and so forth. He was to collect these from his friends and send them to fellow construction workers who were injured on the job. The task was a metaphor for a life's work that had value beyond earning a living; he was to actively seek joy in life through contact with others, and spread joy to those in need.

In another instance, Jay Haley (1993) relates:

> Once many years ago, a research investigator was engaging in long conversations with Erickson to obtain generalizations about his therapeutic procedures. The young man wanted clear statements about his 'method' and Erickson was doing his best to educate him. At a certain point Erickson interrupted the discussion and took the young man outside the house to the front lawn. He pointed up the street and asked what he saw. Puzzled, the young man replied that he saw a street. Erickson asked if he saw anything else. When he continued to be puzzled, Erickson pointed to the trees which lined the street. 'Do you notice anything about those trees?' he asked. After a period of study, the young man said they all were leaning in an easterly direction. 'That's right', said Erickson, pleased. 'All except one. That second one from the end is leaning in a westerly direction. There's always an exception.'

At the time of that incident, I thought that Erickson was going to excessive trouble to make a point; yet now whenever I attempt to simplify complex processes, particularly when describing Erickson's work, the experience in Phoenix that afternoon comes vividly to mind. (Haley, 1993: 36–7)

The simple, but experiential exercise of walking out on the front lawn and requiring the student to be observant was clearly impactful. The exceptional tree served as a powerful symbol for Haley in grappling with generalizations about treatment.

Anecdotes

Quite akin to metaphor, is Erickson's technique of telling anecdotes. Anecdotes are more constrained than metaphors in that the story format of beginning (orientation), middle (account of events) and end (conclusion) is requisite. In contrast, a metaphor, as illustrated above, may be a simple statement or even a puzzle. The anecdote may, however, be a metaphor (symbolic representation) or it can be more directly illustrative. Anecdotes, often case presentations, were commonly used by Erickson in teaching his method to other practitioners.

The telling of stories, or more correctly, the hearing of stories, can evoke an unconscious recollection of childhood, openness and curiosity. It elicits a state of passive attention and facilitates trance induction (can anyone doubt this who has observed a room full of first graders absorbed in a story read aloud?). The anecdote, whether symbolic or more plainly instructive, has the advantage of bypassing resistance, as metaphors do. The anecdote doesn't say to the patient or student, 'You should do "x".' It says instead, 'Here's someone who did "x" and here's what happened.' And in the process of the hearing, an anecdote is more readily internalized than a simple statement. For this reason the fable of 'The Boy Who Cried Wolf' is more compelling than the simple statement 'Don't tell lies to get attention.'

In the next case, anecdotes are used for pain control with a couple.

Treatment

A couple, both of whom were experiencing physical problems, sought treatment from Dr Erickson. The man was experiencing phantom limb pain (sensation in a leg that had been amputated) and his wife had tinnitus (a ringing in the ear). In the course of their conversation, Erickson told the couple about a time when he travelled around as a college student. He stopped at a boiler factory, and asked the foreman whether or not he could spend the night in an out of the way corner. He had to have the man repeat his answer several times in order to hear over the din of production. In the morning, the workers were surprised to find that he could hear their normal conversational tone, since it had taken them much longer to acquire that skill. Erickson said he knew that the body could learn quickly. He went on to tell the couple about a television programme he had seen about nomads, who lived in the Iranian desert. In spite of the climate they wore layers of clothing quite comfortably. During the remainder of the session, he told several more anecdotes, all of which revolved around the theme of the ability to become unaware of an unpleasant constant (Erickson and Rossi, 1979).

Instruction
The following is an anecdote that Erickson told in a teaching situation. It is an excellent example of the instructional (non-treatment) use of storytelling:

> I was returning from high school one day and a runaway horse with a bridle on sped past a group of us into a farmer's yard . . . looking for a drink of water. The horse was perspiring heavily. And the farmer didn't recognize it, so we cornered it. I hopped on the horse's back . . . since it had a bridle on, I took hold of the rein and said, 'Giddy-up' . . . headed for the highway. I knew the horse would turn in the right direction . . . I didn't know what the right direction was. And the horse trotted and galloped along. Now and then he would forget he was on the highway and start into a field. So I would pull on him a bit and call his attention to the fact that the highway was where he was supposed to be. And finally about four miles from where I had boarded him he turned into a farm yard and the farmer said, 'So that's how that critter came back. Where did you find him?' I said, 'About four miles from here.' 'How did you know he should come here?' I said, 'I didn't know . . . the horse knew. All I did was keep his attention on the road.' . . . I think that's the way you do psychotherapy. (O'Hanlon, 1987: 8–9)

Implication

The concept of implication was touched on briefly in the section of this chapter addressing metaphors. Implication is a method of communication in which an idea is suggested without directly saying it. Once the reader understands the value of this particular kind of communication, he or she will also realize why it was used so frequently by Erickson. It permitted him to progress in the therapy process with the implied portion as a foregone conclusion that did not need to be laboriously established. Again, like metaphors and anecdotes, this technique is not directly confrontive to the patient's perception, and thus engenders little resistance. It suggests possibilities without asserting certainty. For example, the third sentence in this paragraph implies that the reader *will* understand the value of this technique. This may or may not happen, but we are permitted to proceed as if it will, which creates an atmosphere conducive to that outcome.

Applications

A common use of implication is in trance induction. The hypnotist might mention, during that process, that he or she is uncertain whether it is those fluttering eyelids which will close first, or the respiration which will slow sooner. It is implied that one of the two will happen first and that both will happen. Such unusual language forms faster absorption and dissociative response, both of which are central to hypnotic phenomenology.

Once Erickson (Haley, 1973: 197–8) was asked by a concerned mother to help with her daughter who was becoming withdrawn and isolative owing to embarrassment from her belief that her feet were too large. Erickson carefully contrived to have the girl be present to assist (fetch towels, etc.) while he examined the mother. Then, at the end of the examination, while absorbed in talking to mother, he 'accidentally' stepped down hard on the girl's toes. He turned angrily and said 'If you'd just grow those things large enough for a man to see, I wouldn't be in this sort of situation.' The girl was on her way to a movie with a friend before Erickson left their home, and the pattern of isolation was ended. The implication – that her feet were *small* – was delivered in such a way that it could not be construed as a false compliment or consolation.

In another case, a man came to see Erickson (Haley, 1973: 247–9) because he was troubled over ongoing conflicts with his wife. During his discourse he described how it was that, while he was away on business, his wife would get lonesome and one of his friends would come by to keep her company, leaving at dinnertime. He was pleased that his wife wouldn't have to be lonely. Once he found a tube of toothpaste left there by a friend, another time a used razor blade different from his own. He described how she had gotten pubic lice doing social work with the poor. Finally, about five hours into his discourse, he said, 'You know, if my wife was any other woman, I'd say she was having affairs.' Erickson asked 'In what way does your wife differ from other women?' At that point the denial broke, and the man said what Erickson only implied, 'My God, my wife *is* any other woman.' A direct assault on his denial might well have caused defensiveness, but patience, and the implication that his wife *was* like other women, broke through.

Paradoxical Intervention

A missionary found himself confronted by a tribe of cannibals, who prized, above all else, truth and their integrity. They told the missionary that he would have the opportunity to make a statement, and thereby determine his manner of death – quickly, by spear, if his statement was truth, or painfully, boiled in oil, if he lied. The missionary was silent, thinking, then made his statement. They let him go free. His response had created a paradox – 'You will kill me by boiling me in oil.' Either manner of death would have made liars of his captors, so they were compelled to free him.

There is both a contradiction and truth present in any paradox, which seems to confound reason in a way that disrupts one's ordinary, linear sense of the world. In that moment of disruption, a person is open to a therapeutic perceptual reorganization. Erickson loved these pattern disruptions and used them liberally. For example, he might send the parents of a reluctant child out of his office, scornfully condemning to the child their nerve at telling *him* to cure the child, *Who did they think they were?*, etc. In so doing, he joined the child in being indignant, both winning the child's confidence and assuring the child that he wouldn't *make* the child do anything. From this position of opposition to the parents, he would then proceed to accompany the child through the process of curing their bed-wetting, thumb sucking or nail biting, which was the end the parents had hoped for all along.

There are two types of paradoxical approach – symptom prescription and binds. Symptom prescription is paradoxical in that it seems to get to the right place by going farther in the wrong direction, and binds are paradoxical because they create the sort of internal logical conflict presented at the outset of this section. Perhaps these interventions are effective because they resonate with the internal inconsistencies present within all of us.

Symptom Prescription

One variety of symptom prescription was described above in the way that Erickson often dealt with resistant child patients. The detailed account of dealing with the heckler (see pp. 44–5) is yet another example of how encouraging opposition was utilized in a positive manner. In these cases the message was 'Be this oppositional way of yours, but accomplish your desired behaviour.'

An adolescent girl (Erickson, 1958) who sucked her thumb in a loud and apparently obnoxious way had resisted parents, teachers, peers and her church in their efforts to get her to stop. Erickson extracted a commitment from the parents to co-operate with therapy fully for a month, and to keep any disapproval to themselves. He then took the girl as a patient and encouraged that if she were going to be aggressive (annoying) with her thumb sucking, she ought to do it really well. He told her how: she was to sit by her father as he read the evening paper and suck loudly for no less than 20 minutes, then go and do the same thing next to mother as she sewed. She also was to give a healthy dose of that to any peers or teachers she disliked or who disliked her. Within four weeks, the behaviour diminished, then disappeared, to be replaced by healthier social interests.

Erickson (1954a) worked with an adolescent retarded boy who had developed a compulsive movement and anaesthesia in his right arm. The movements were counted and found to be 135 times per minute. It was suggested to the boy that he increase these to 145 per minute for the period between sessions, which he did. At the next session the frequency was reduced, only to be increased at the following session. Thus, in a step-wise, up-a-little-and-down-more fashion, the frequency of arm movements was eventually decreased to five per minute. Thereafter, fluctuating frequency was measured in movements per day, then movements per week. The anaesthesia increased and decreased along with arm movements. At last the boy was given a chance to guess when the movements would stop for a whole day, then for good. The boy guessed correctly.

The applications for symptom prescription are far-ranging – symptom prescription may be used in individual, couples or family therapy. In the first example, the encouraged increase in thumb sucking gave the girl plenty of time to consider whether she chose to continue or not. The suggested increase in the second case illustrates how a perceived inability to control a compulsion is disrupted when a person learns that choosing to do *more* means they can also choose to do less.

Binds

A woman came to see Dr Erickson (Rossi *et al.*, 1983: 270–1) with a concern that she would die at the age of 22 of heart disease, as her mother, grandmother and great-grandmother all had done. In recounting the preparations she had been making for her death, she noted that she was keeping all of her bills paid up because she certainly was not going to leave any unpaid bills behind. In trance, among other things, she agreed with Erickson's speculation that, had her mother and grandmother lived to be 23, then they probably would have lived a lot longer. She also agreed with him that any business had the right to name the date of payment for their bill. At the close of the session, he informed her that he expected to be paid in exactly 14 months, which happened to be her 23rd birthday. She showed up as scheduled to pay.

In a more personal example, Erickson told of the day one of his sons stated he wouldn't eat any spinach. Erickson heartily agreed, stating that he didn't believe the child was old enough, big enough or strong enough to eat any. Mrs Erickson argued that the child was big enough. The boy, of course, took his mother's side. Mother and son disputed Erickson's proposed compromise that a half teaspoon would be enough, so they settled on a half dish. The child ate that quickly and demanded more, again with mother's support. Erickson reluctantly agreed that maybe the boy was bigger than he first thought (Erickson and Rossi, 1975).

In this instance, Erickson's agreement that the child should not have spinach was predicated on his stated perception of the boy as too little. In order for the boy to continue agreeing with 'no spinach' he had to agree with an image of self as too little. Conversely, eating the spinach enhanced the more positive 'big boy' image in his and his father's eyes. This is vastly different from the pop psychology technique of 'reverse psychology'. In the first example, Erickson pitted the woman's values (don't leave unpaid bills) and sense of right (a business can set time of payment) against her long held belief that she would die at 22 years. She could not die at 22 and be true to two of her beliefs. The usefulness of the bind is so apparent that it has become part of our culture. It is common in even basic parenting skills training: Offer your child choices, 'Will you brush your teeth *before* or *after* your bath?', 'Do you want a few green beans or a lot?'

Task Assignments

Erickson recognized that often a behavioural change precedes psychological change. It was, therefore, common for him to pre-scribe a task (most often performed outside of the session) in order to achieve a desired outcome. One can think of these tasks as being of at least four types; problem-oriented, skill building, ordeal and ambiguous function assignments. As suggested earlier in this chapter, for Erickson, a given intervention was seldom one tech-nique, but more frequently a custom built, hybrid, one-of-a-kind amalgamation of techniques appropriate only for that patient and that problem. This was true of a large percentage of Erickson's task assignments. It can be noted here that, as an exception, a significant number of people were given the same directive (to climb Squaw Peak, which is a well-traversed mountain in Phoenix – a fit climber takes less than one hour for a round trip), though the reason for the assignment varied from person to person. This will be discussed further in the Ambiguous Function Assignments section.

Problem-oriented Tasks

A woman came to see Erickson because she wanted to lose weight and quit smoking. She said, 'I can't resist eating and I can't resist smoking, but I can resist exercise, and I do.' Erickson learned that she was religious and so extracted her most solemn promise that she would follow his instructions. She lived in a two storey house. Whenever she wanted a cigarette, she was to go to the basement where she kept her matches and set one on top of the box. Then she was to run up to the attic where she would keep her cigarettes, then run back down to the basement to light and smoke it. If she wanted some cake, she was to cut a thin slice, then run around the outside of her house before she ate it. If she wanted a second slice, she was to cut a thin one, then run around the house *two* times before eating it, and so forth. Soon she cut down on cigarettes and began reducing nicely (Zeig, 1980: 195).

In another instance, a couple married for a year came to see Erickson because the wife had bitter feelings toward her husband. It seems that her husband got an erection just going to the bedroom and getting into bed at night, and he awoke with one in the morning. She was frustrated, explaining 'If once, just once, he would get into bed and not be able to have an erection automatically . . . if just once he could let me feel my female power.' It was important to her that something other than just looking at her or being in the bedroom was responsible for his arousal; she wanted to evoke the response. With the wife out of the room, Erickson educated the husband about the importance of this, and instructed the man to climb into bed that night with a flaccid penis. This was assured through repeated masturbation prior to bed time. The wife had a delightful time in arousing her husband that night and gained a real sense of her female power. She also lost her bitterness toward her husband (Haley, 1973: 159).

In these two cases, the tasks that Erickson required fit the therapeutic need in a straightforward, common sense way. Therefore, we called these 'problem-oriented task assignments'. It is sufficient to note that the patient in the first example was *not* told 'Don't smoke, eat less', she was told to do as she pleased, but to do it in a particular way. In the other example, the instruction to arrive in bed with a flaccid penis is so simple as to have one wonder whether it qualifies as therapy. Yet one cannot doubt that it was therapeutic, given that the couple's conflict abated. The true beauty of this technique is in its economy of treatment. Contrast this single session intervention with, for example, months or even years of protracted couples' treatment.

Skill Building

A 70-year-old woman called Ma Kate presented a great challenge to Erickson. Her parents had not believed in education for women, and though she seemed quite bright, she had remained illiterate all of her life. For 50 years, prior to meeting Erickson, she had taken in local school teachers as boarders at reduced rates with the agreement that they would teach her to read and write. And for 50 years those teachers tried in vain and eventually gave up. Hearing a detailed history of these efforts, Erickson concluded that Ma Kate had a psychological block that might yield to hypnotherapy. He not only agreed to teach her to read, but to do so in three weeks! His work with her most often began in hypnosis, and was then repeated in the waking state. He told her that she would have to learn nothing that she did not already know, but she would only need to do things she had learned long ago. First he had her hold a pencil however she liked, and make a scribble on a paper. Next a straight line, like making a mark on a board with a nail prior to cutting. She was instructed to draw a vertical, horizontal and slanting straight line. Then a mark like a doughnut hole, then a half doughnut, and the other half. She was sent away to practise all these marks.

At the next session she was told that the only difference between a pile of lumber and a completed house was that the house was the lumber put together. As the process continued, she used the letter parts (lines, circles, semi-circles) she had learned to draw, to form letters, although she was not told they were letters. These letters were described in terms of items she already knew (e.g. the letter 'L' being a carpenter's square standing on the short leg). She was thus guided first through forming letters, then words. As these were specific combinations she was building, she also had to learn to 'name' them, and she learned that naming them was just like talking. Thus, bit by bit, she put together what she already knew and, astonishingly, inside of three weeks was reading (Erickson, 1959a).

This case demonstrates the essence of skill-building tasks, and emanates from the principle that patients already have the resources to solve their problem. The therapeutic objective, then, is to find the way to develop skill-building task assignments that systematically build upon the resource base in an incremental manner to achieve the desired outcome. The principle of building in increments allowed Erickson to assist a high school shotputter to find his way past the 58-foot limit that his throws had reached. Erickson wondered whether the boy could really tell the difference between 58 feet and 58-1/100 feet. Could he possibly put the shot 1/100th feet further? 3/100th? and so forth. The lad broke the national high school record three weeks later. During his career he advanced the world record by 6 feet 10 inches (Rosen, 1982: 102–5).

Ordeals

Some of the tasks that Dr Erickson prescribed were so detailed, lengthy and/or laborious as to be termed 'ordeals'. An ordeal might involve only an individual (as in the 'sleep or work' case cited in Chapter 2, p. 36) or multiple family members. While the ordeal may serve multiple functions, one quality of the process is that giving up the symptom or problem behaviour is clearly superior to continuing the ordeal.

A boy had a nasty ulcer on his forehead from picking at a pimple and never allowing it to heal. The self-abuse had continued for two years and had not yielded to lectures, medical advice and treatment (including bandages), threats, teasing by schoolmates, and even unreasonable punishments. The boy felt that this was a bad habit he could not break. Erickson, as always, did his homework, and learned that the boy was having spelling problems because he often left letters out of words. He also learned which weekend chores belonged to the boy. Having obtained a commitment from the family, he prescribed the task. The boy was to spend Saturdays and Sundays from 6:00 a.m. until late afternoon working on his *handwriting* – filling up page after page with the sentence, 'It is not a good idea to pick at that sore on my forehead.' This sentence, incidentally, was one that the boy selected to write through negotiation with Erickson. He was to examine his work carefully and count each letter. He was to notice which ones he did best, and where he could do better. While he was doing this, father was given responsibility for the boy's chores. During his breaks, he could go and inspect how father was coming along in doing his chores for him. To be sure, he delighted in finding even a leaf out of place in the yard.

Within a month, the ulcer healed. The yard never looked better. The boy's writing and spelling improved. Penmanship, in fact, became the focus of the ordeal: 'You have a bad habit – of dropping letters out of words.' The child and his family were committed to overcoming a bad habit – they overcame two in the process (Haley, 1985c: 100–4).

Ambiguous Function Assignment

In the introductory section about task assignments we noted that Erickson often sent people to climb Squaw Peak. This was occasionally an ambiguous function assignment. (See Lankton and Lankton, 1983, for more information.) In some ways, ambiguous tasks may be the most ingenious of Erickson's interventions, and the most pure in that they rely so heavily on the patient as a source. These assignments have no readily apparent meaning or intent, and so become a sort of behavioural projective technique – what patients experience is what they bring with them, and perhaps what they need to learn.

The following case involves the use of tasks that are metaphoric and ambiguous:

A psychiatrist and his wife travelled from Pennsylvania for marital therapy. They gave a brief account of their circumstances – he had a stagnant practice which he neglected, and had been in analysis three times a week for 13 years; she worked at a job she didn't like, to help support them, and had been in analysis three times a week for six years. Erickson sent the man to climb Squaw Peak, to spend three hours doing it, and report back the next day. The woman was sent with similar instructions to the Desert Botanical Gardens.

The next day, the man reported that his experience was wonderful. The woman reported that her three hours at the Botanical Gardens were the most boring of her life, and she would never go back. Then, the wife was sent to climb Squaw Peak and the husband to visit the Botanical Gardens. The next morning, the psychiatrist reported how marvellous all the diversity of plant life was in thriving in the brutal Arizona heat with little water. He found it inspiring. The wife said to Erickson, 'I climbed that God-damned mountain. I swore at that mountain. I swore at myself, but mostly I swore at you all the way up with every step. I wonder why I was such a damn fool that I would climb that mountain. Boring. I hated myself for doing it. But, because you said I should, I did. I got to the top. For a few minutes, I felt a feeling of satisfaction, but it didn't last very long. And I cursed at you and myself more thoroughly every step of the way down. I swore I would never, never again climb a mountain like that and make such a fool of myself.'

That afternoon, each could choose their own task, and they were to report back the next morning. The husband reported that he returned to the gardens and again found it enjoyable. The wife, amazingly, had elected to once again climb Squaw Peak. She didn't like it any better the second time, and cursed Erickson, the mountain, and herself the whole way up and down. With that, Dr Erickson informed them that their treatment was complete, and sent them back to Pennsylvania. Upon returning home, each fired their analyst. Husband began tending to his practice. Wife got a lawyer and divorced her husband. She got a different job more to her liking and became much happier. In Erickson's words, 'She got tired of climbing that mountain of marital distress day after day . . . Her whole story was a symbolic report.' An interesting footnote to this case is that the couple's analyst and his wife later came to Erickson for marital therapy. (Zeig, 1980: 146)

Non-compliance

On occasion, as suggested elsewhere in this text, a patient would decide that he or she was unwilling to follow through with a given assignment. Just as the ambiguous function assignment offered a certain amount of insight into the patient since it served as a projective technique, a patient's manner of responding (or failure to follow through) on any task assignment yields information about the patient and his attitude toward treatment.

An overweight woman came to Erickson asking for assistance in reducing. He instructed her to climb Squaw Peak at sunrise, and she asked whether or not she could take her son along, who also happened to be overweight. When she returned for her next session, she reported that neither of them had made the climb. She asked Erickson if it was all right if she quit fooling herself about wanting to lose weight, and he told her that he didn't mind at all (Rosen, 1982: 126–7).

This case is an excellent example of a therapeutic outcome, even with failure to comply; it produced an awareness in the patient that she was really not ready to do the work to lose the weight. This insight spared the patient a good deal of effort and discomfort that, in all likelihood, would have failed to result in weight loss, and also would have served to convince her further of the impossibility of ever reducing. In this case she never failed because she chose not to try.

Conclusion

The authors would be pleased to state here that this chapter has provided a thorough overview of all of Milton Erickson's technical contributions to the field of psychotherapy. It has not. No single chapter, or book, could adequately achieve that. Erickson's interventions, to be redundant, were unique for each patient. His own technical repertoire was vast and he had the resources of his patients upon which to draw. None-the-less, this chapter has reviewed a number of important, unique technical contributions that Erickson made to the field of psychotherapy.

In the broadest of terms, his most important technical contribution has been in the domain of hypnosis – he can be credited with legitimizing the practice of clinical hypnosis. His interest in hypnosis resulted in a significant contribution to the scientific research and clinical literature on hypnosis and hypnotic phenomena. He adapted many phenomena to the therapy process, and even developed phenomena that had not previously been observed (e.g. arm levitation). His true mastery of the process even allowed him to use the pantomime technique successfully to hypnotize a naive subject who had no expectations that she would be hypnotized, and shared no common language with Erickson.

Erickson also developed a number of 'non-hypnotic techniques', such as the use of metaphor, anecdotes, double binds, paradoxical interventions, implication and task assignments. These techniques fit well with a symptom-focused, brief approach, and of course, lend themselves to an orientation that prizes the notion of utilizing any aspect of the patient and/or his life in service of problem resolution.

Within the framework of hypnotic intervention are a number of techniques developed by Dr Erickson that are too advanced for discussion in an introductory text. The interspersal technique, the confusion technique, and the hypnotically induced dream are examples of his work that are appropriate for discussion in an advanced hypnosis training seminar. For similar reasons, we have declined to discuss, in any depth, such complex concepts as multiple embedded metaphor, and the use of symbols, which are advanced technical developments that can be used either with or without hypnosis.

While we have been unable to completely catalogue all of his technical innovations here, the present chapter will certainly give the reader a clear sense of the scope of Erickson's technical contributions. While these innovations continue to gain broader acceptance, and the philosophy that drives them is embraced by an increasingly large number of practitioners, it is axiomatic that innovation breeds criticism. In the next chapter we will examine the most cogent of these critical evaluations.

Notes

1. An elaborate explication of Erickson's technique in this case is found in an appendix of *A Teaching Seminar with Milton H. Erickson* (Zeig, 1980).
2. The answer is a five-pointed star.

4

Criticisms and Rebuttals

> I think any theoretically-based psychotherapy is mistaken because each person is different.
>
> Milton H. Erickson (Zeig, 1980: 131)

This chapter reviews and examines the validity of the criticisms most commonly levelled at Milton H. Erickson's work. In what might be considered an Ericksonian perspective, it is suggested at the outset that each of these criticisms is simultaneously both valid and invalid. The following two descriptions provide illustrations.

Strengths

The Ericksonian approach identifies the strengths, resources and unique aspects of each patient which are then incorporated into problem resolution; it is free of rigid theoretical constraints which define and limit the therapist's vision of the patient. The patient's unconscious mind is a powerful ally in providing both corrective information and in effecting solutions. Therefore, brief treatment is possible, often without the necessity of developing insight; the identified problem is relieved and patients are free to go about the business of living their life free from time-consuming psychotherapy.

The resources of the practitioner also facilitate problem resolution. Milton Erickson was a superlative clinician who developed excellent rapport with his patients and was able to join them in their phenomenological worlds. His perceptiveness and ingenuity enhanced his therapeutic effectiveness immeasurably.

Weakness

The Ericksonian therapeutic approach lacks a theoretical framework and is therefore neither readily researched nor taught. There are no set protocols to guide the inexperienced clinician in developing interventions. Some interventions utilize the patient's unconscious mind beyond that patient's awareness; this seems manipulative and may compromise informed consent. Interventions often are directive, and are thus subject to possible therapist bias and abuse. Critics contend that since insight is often not primary, changes that result from treatment are superficial. They opine that Erickson was charismatic and a cult figure who exercised undue control over his patients; only he could do what he did.

Half Empty or Half Full?

Both the strengths and weaknesses delineated above have some validity. Each of the preceding sections sequentially addresses similar aspects of the approach, but from a different perspective. For example, the atheoretical nature of the approach, which allows it to develop unique interventions for each patient, also renders it less amenable to standardized research and teaching methods.

It was suggested in the initial paragraph that regarding these criticisms as both valid and invalid would be an 'Ericksonian' thing to do. Indeed, the ability to find the strength in the weakness, the solution in the problem, and the curative paradox in the patient's situation was part and parcel of Erickson's genius in assisting patients.

The Criticisms

The remainder of this chapter examines in detail the most common criticisms of Erickson's approach. With a few exceptions, these criticisms can be broadly grouped into four clusters. The *theoretical criticisms* result from the atheoretical nature of the approach, and hold that:

1. there is a paucity of research;
2. it is difficult to learn the approach;
3. inexperienced clinicians do not get a protocol or clear treatment model.

The *ethical criticisms* state that:

4. the approach is manipulative;
5. it gives directives;
6. the technique is superficial.

The *personal criticisms* suggest that:

7. Erickson is a cult figure;
8. the therapist must be charismatic, so that only Erickson could do what he did.

The *approach limitations* are criticisms that suggest that:

9. the approach only works with certain patient populations;
10. the therapist needs a lot of patients to make a living.

Assessing the Validity of any Criticism

In a chapter dedicated to examining what others have suggested are negative aspects of Erickson's work, it is useful to examine the context and nature of criticism as it occurs in regard to psychotherapy approaches in general. There are a variety of psychotherapeutic approaches that are commonly accepted practice, including psycho-analysis, cognitive approaches, cognitive/behavioural approaches, behavioural, client centred, gestalt, existential and group therapy. Each offers something that the others do not, and whatever that 'something' is, sets the approach apart and gives it an identity that is linked to its unique contribution. This essential difference is measured in terms of how the approach varies from standard or accepted practice. It is also a double edged sword – something is lost and something gained by virtue of the difference(s).

An approach may differ from accepted practice by doing some-thing that might be considered to be inappropriate (commission), or conversely by not doing something that is considered to be crucial (omission). For example, Alexander Lowen's Bio-energetic Approach entails extensive therapist/patient physical contact, which is pro-hibited in many other approaches. Similarly, brief approaches such as Solution-focused Treatment may elicit functional change without fostering insight. Since insight development is considered to be essential in psychodynamic approaches, those who prize insight may label brief approaches as deficient.

While there is at least some basis in reality for most criticisms, the evaluation may be tainted if it comes from a self-serving perspective. These evaluations are often either incomplete in scope, or draw erroneous conclusions. All major approaches are open to criticism based on the same logical type of error, which is to identify the characteristics of the approach that set it apart from all others, and then discount it for acts of commission or omission secondary to those differences. For example, critics of behavioural (learning theory-based) approaches often suggest that the theory is reductionistic in scope; that it fails to recognize the free will of the individual as a self-regulating mediator of behaviour; and that since insight does not develop, symptom substitution is likely to occur. In fact, it is the reductionistic nature of the theory that allows for development of interventions that are simple, effective, and both replicable and measurable. The criticism of the reductionistic nature of the approach fails to provide a complete picture of the *value* of the reductionistic aspect. Similarly, the conclusion that symptom substitution will occur is erroneous. Kazdin (1982) reviewed the literature and found general agreement that the empirical phenomena of symptom substitution (replacement of a treated symptom with another, noxious symptom) has been documented in individual cases. He concludes, however, that strong evidence attesting to the appearance of substitute symptoms after psychotherapy or behaviour therapy is hard to find. As far as insight is concerned, Cautela (1993) has written about spontaneous, and even therapist guided instances of insight development occurring within the context of Behaviour Therapy.

There are, of course, valid criticisms that examine the full scope and impact of the approach, and draw thoughtful conclusions. Electro-convulsive Shock Treatment (ECT) is an example of a treatment that, in decades past, was often used for profoundly disturbed patients. Breggin (1979) has examined the negative impact of ECT, and found permanent retrograde amnesia to be the most common side effect, along with anterograde mental impairment. In the years since, these valid concerns have been the impetus for careful study and refinement in the use of this intervention.

As we examine the various concerns surrounding Erickson's approach, we will (as he certainly would have done) proceed in our evaluation with an eye toward the evidence and completeness of the critique.

Theoretical Criticisms

The Ericksonian approach is atheoretical, and is therefore subject, at least on the surface, to the criticism that it is lacking in the strengths that are derived from a strong theoretical base. Specifically, an approach with a well-defined theory lends itself to scientific research, the theory provides a conceptual framework that can be easily learned, and the conceptual framework lends itself to the development of contingent protocols. The absence of theory-based strengths gives rise to the criticisms that Ericksonian methods cannot be researched, that the approach is difficult to learn, and that there are no protocols to assist the novice Ericksonian practitioner.

Erickson eschewed theory in the practice of psychotherapy as limiting and confining. Indeed, it was Erickson's aim to create a new intervention for each patient. He maintained that the most effective intervention strategy for a given patient was the one that best matched the patient's needs and utilized the patient's unique assets. Conceptually, this orientation is the polar opposite of *any* theoretical approach, which is based on the assumption of common process among individuals. Random House Dictionary (1994) defines theory as 'A coherent group of general propositions used as principles of explanation for a class of phenomena.' In order for a theory of psychotherapy to be applicable, members of a class or subclass (patients) must be regarded as similar. Theory bound approaches assume commonality among class members (e.g. psychoanalysis presupposes that all patients progress through the same series of developmental stages; behavioural approaches assume that a given problematic behaviour is a response to a specific conditioned stimulus or class of stimuli; and so forth).

Research

The conceptual standardization of class members (in our case, patients) permits theory to delineate consistent explanatory principles, and these principles, by virtue of their repetitive and predictable nature, permit research. Ironically, in spite of his refusal to adhere to a theory of psychotherapy, Erickson was a dedicated researcher who sought ways of testing and validating ideas from the time he was a boy. During his tenure at Eloise Hospital in Michigan, he was Director of Research. The first 'stage' of his career was as a researcher, followed by his periods as a clinician and teacher. While Erickson was accomplished in the use of classical experimental methodology, he researched hypnotic phenomena more like an anthropologist than an empiricist. He explored individual differences rather than group norms, which was in keeping with his emphasis on the uniqueness of the person.

Erickson maintained that much of what he did clinically, could not be examined through traditional experimental methods, owing to the individual differences of patients, or in the laboratory, subjects. His focus on the unique qualities of subjects can be seen in a statement he made during a round table discussion on hypnosis (Erickson, circa 1960; also in Rossi, 1980b).

> I have nothing to add to the general understanding of how to induce a trance except to stress the importance of making full provision for all individual differences and peculiarities of the subject and the highly personal character of the hypnotic relationship. . . .
>
> Later in that meeting, he commented on standardized inductions: . . . we find quantitative studies made of hypnotic phenomena by controlling the suggestions given by use of a certain phonograph record *as if such a measure could control the nature and extent of the development of the response processes so aroused in different subjects.* (p. 304; emphasis added)

Erickson's belief that neither hypnotic subjects nor psychotherapy patients could effectively be treated in a standardized way, led him to adopt a different research method. Dating back to his first year of experimentation with hypnosis, Erickson kept records of his work with subjects. These were field notes that recorded methods of trance induction as well as trance phenomena elicited. He summarized these and reported them to the graduate seminar he attended with Clark Hull.

Rossi (1980a) noted that Erickson thought of most of his hypno-therapeutic work as experimental and exploratory in nature. He also regarded trance responsiveness as idiosyncratic, which means that the hypnotist must be vigilant and attentive to the unique spontaneous emergence of various trance phenomena. Over the years, he kept copious records and accounts of phenomena that he observed and replicated. His method of field observation was one of the ways that Erickson researched patient responsiveness in therapy.

In order to conduct more traditional research, Erickson (circa 1960) believed that it was essential to distinguish between experimentally and clinically satisfactory trance states. Experimental trance states, characterized as more profound, differed from clinical trances in terms of depth of subject involvement. The experimental subject is responsive to suggestion, but merely incorporates the suggestion into the ongoing subjective experience, which is internally generated and may be beyond the control of the hypnotist. By way of example, Erickson (circa 1960) told of a young man who, in trance, was reliving the experience of driving his milk route. The lad delayed, waiting for a flock of geese to finish crossing in front of his milk wagon. Erickson, who was unaware of the halucinated geese, suggested that the horse pulling the wagon would continue on its way, only to find that the subject was compelled to rein in the horse before it trampled the geese. The subject incorporated Erickson's suggestion, but not at the expense of fully modifying his own internal experience.

In contradistinction, in the clinically satisfactory trance, the subject or patient is responsive to the hypnotist and will modify the internal experience according to suggestion. Erickson believed that a lot of what passed for legitimate research really relied on subjects who were in clinically responsive trance states, and were therefore responsive to verbal and non-verbal experimenter expectation. Investigations utilizing subjects with this level of responsiveness obviously could produce tainted results.

The problem of experimenter bias secondary to expectation was validated in a study utilizing subjects who routinely developed experimentally suitable trance states. They were hypnotized and given the instruction to respond fully to the instructions they received, and to *meet the expectations* of the students giving the instructions. Students were given a variety of possible suggestion phrases from which to select, and a set of target phenomena, all of which they were to elicit from the hypnotic subjects. The hypnotic subjects were competent in all of the trance phenomena involved (e.g. arm levitation and hallucination). The students giving the instructions were divided into experimental groups, with each group being led to believe that their hypnotic subject was competent in all but one hypnotic phenomenon, which varied across groups. The result was that the hypnotic subjects met the unspoken expectation of the students, and failed to produce only the specific phenomena at which the students believed them to be incompetent (Erickson, 1960).

The experimenter bias study reported above is an example of Erickson's type of research which consisted of field experiments and clinical observations. Recognizing the impossibility of applying traditional research methods to his clinical work, Erickson found other methods of evaluating his work; he routinely made long-term follow-up a part of his intervention. The literature is replete with instances of checking in on a patient repeatedly over the course of months and even years. In *An Uncommon Casebook*, O'Hanlon and Hexum (1990) not only catalogue and summarize 316 case studies, they list the outcome and follow-up interval data which is available for most cases.

The criticism that much of Erickson's approach cannot be empirically researched is partially valid. Erickson, however, demonstrated that with creativity and ingenuity, some of the phenomena with which he worked can be subjected to empirical validation. In fact his contribution to the literature on research of hypnosis and hypnotic phenomena is outstanding. He also made a substantial contribution in terms of published clinical case studies. Finally, since the approach is change oriented, any intervention is geared toward producing a specific, planned outcome that can be compared with the actual result. Anyone practising the Ericksonian approach can readily compare their intended result with the actual outcome. This is known as research with $N = 1$, and is a recommended practice that is available to any clinician utilizing any approach.

Learning

The Ericksonian approach has been criticized as being difficult to learn since it lacks a theoretical base – there is no conceptual structure upon which to build an understanding of the methods. The absence of theory, however, has not deterred practitioners from learning and practising the Ericksonian approach. There are guiding principles (see Chapter 2) that assist in conceptualizing the process. Our goal in this section is to examine the learning process as it relates to the concept of theory. What is a theory?

Theory is by its nature an intellectual exercise. It is a paradigm designed to assist in organizing thinking about a complex process, and, ultimately, to assist in formulating predictions. As a model, it is a description of reality as understood at a given point in time, and therefore subject to change if a new set of facts emerge that do not fit the theory.

If one wishes to examine the relative merits of having or not having a guiding theory in learning the practice of psychotherapy, then one must examine what is gained and what is lost through adherence to a given theory. Simple articulation (and therefore discussion), specified process and specific treatment protocols are the benefits derived from clearly defined theories, and research is therefore simpler and more definitive. Erickson argued that adherence to a theory always closed down treatment options by defining where the therapist gives (and does not give) his/her attention; that theories fail to adequately respect the uniqueness of each patient; and most importantly, that the implicit expectation is that the theory is the source of the problem resolution, as opposed to the meaningful resources brought to the therapy encounter by the patient. These are the costs of adherence to a theory; Erickson contended that the cost was too high.

Consider an analogy from everyday life. Most people can ride a bicycle. This is a skill that is acquired experientially. Bicycle riding is also an exercise in applied physics, although most people ride bikes without ever being able to articulate the specific principles involved. A competent physicist, however, could delineate the underlying principles, building them into a coherent theory of how to ride a bike down a street, executing turns, and safely avoiding parked cars. Not only would such a theory lack much practical value, such a theory would be rendered completely useless in the case of mountain biking, which is perhaps a more fitting analogy for the therapeutic challenges that face most practitioners on a daily basis.

Erickson's students learned through doing, through experiencing. They were hypnotized, told stories, sent for walks through the Botanical Gardens and up Squaw Peak, they watched demonstrations, solved puzzles and word games. They had *experiences*! They learned in much the same way that Erickson's patients were treated. Their strengths were utilized and the metaphors given to them for educational purposes were personally relevant.

The criticism in question is that this approach is difficult to learn. This may be so. One may leave the learning experience without a clearly delineated intellectual conceptualization. Yet the experiential base is invaluable, and perhaps more readily accessible in the therapy setting since it doesn't require patients to adhere to any rigid set of principles.

As a final note, it is useful to acknowledge that most approaches to therapy are difficult to learn. Also, it is impossible to parcel out the relative value of the theoretical learning from the experiential learning that is part of indoctrination into any approach. This raises the question of whether it is really familiarity with the theoretical underpinnings, or, in fact, the seven years of personal psychoanalysis that make a psychoanalyst effective.

Protocols

Some critics point out that the Ericksonian approach provides no clear treatment protocols to guide clinicians – this is true. Indeed, Erickson took great pains to declare that 'Psychotherapy for patient "X" is NOT psychotherapy for patient "Y"'. When confronted with a problem such as panic disorder, he eschewed going through sequential treatment steps. He reasoned that any protocol fails to take into consideration the individual patient's abilities, strengths and resources. Any treatment protocol focuses on the identified symptoms as opposed to the whole patient. Protocols fail to examine the systemic function of the symptom(s). They are akin to delivering every baby with forceps. With protocols, an individual is treated as if he or she were no different from any one else, which may well engender resistance and confound the healing process. Treatment protocols are antithetical to an Ericksonian philosophy.

The student of Ericksonian treatment is not, however, without guidance. This book, which is in no manner intended to be a therapy manual, has described six overarching principles, along with an overview of hypnosis and its application, and a review of several other techniques. There are more than 100 other books about Erickson and his work. A system of more than 75 Institutes worldwide sponsors training in Ericksonian approaches. The Milton H. Erickson Foundation in Phoenix provides intensive training modules, lasting five days, that are geared for beginning, intermediate or advanced Ericksonian practitioners. Many acknowledged experts travel worldwide to provide training for professionals.

In all of this vast array of learning opportunities, the novice practitioner repeatedly will get the single most important message: pay close attention to your patient who is the unique source of your understanding of the problem, of the phenomenology, of the innate resources, of the preparedness for change, and of the state of responsiveness. If the practitioner orients to individual differences, keeps in mind the principles mentioned in Chapter 2, and develops familiarity with the array of techniques developed by Erickson, then effective intervention will be greatly facilitated.

Stated succinctly, *the* patient *is the driving force in the treatment selection process – not the symptom, not a theory, and not therapist preferences.* In essence, the foregoing statement *is* a treatment model, that differs from other models in terms of its 'process'. Other models provide the practitioner with an expectation – Rational Emotive Behaviour Therapy (a cognitive behavioural model) enjoins the therapist to look for specific thinking styles that mediate both emotional response and consequent behaviour; Systematic Desensitization (a behavioural approach) tells the therapist to ferret out a graded hierarchy of stimuli that are triggering the anxiety response, then provides a treatment regimen. The Ericksonian model tells the therapist not what to expect, but where to look. The therapy is focused through the unique experiential patterns of the patient.

Again, a criticism of this method is that novice practitioners are not provided protocols or a clear cut treatment model. Given the philosophy of the approach, protocols and simple paradigms are impossible. The Ericksonian method is, however, an approach that is in essence broadly applicable; and simplicity lost is the price paid for that range of applicability.

Ethical Criticisms

There are criticisms that suggest that the Ericksonian approach is, at least in some aspects, ethically suspect. Specifically, it is maintained that the approach is manipulative, directive and superficial. The first two are criticisms of commission (i.e. there are things that the approach does that are prohibited in some theoretical schemas). Superficiality, more an act of omission, is a reflection of the belief that in some way the approach fails to do something that is deemed to be essential to providing complete treatment.

Overview
Any approach has specified standards for treatment. Standards for the approach delimit what can be done within the confines of the approach. In its departure from widely accepted treatment approaches, Ericksonian treatment does violate some of the dictums and requirements of those approaches. One must then evaluate whether or not those specific violations harm or, in fact, help the patient – whether or not they simply reflect a different philosophy of problem resolution. Again, Lowen's Bioenergetic Analysis is an

example of an approach that vastly oversteps the bounds of physical contact as delineated in a psychoanalytic approach, yet patients continue to benefit from this approach with no apparent ill effects resulting from the physical contact. That same degree of contact, occurring in the context of psychoanalysis, would so damage the requisite nature of the patient/analyst relationship that effective analysis might thereafter be rendered impossible.

Beyond this approach specific perspective, however, are ethical considerations that are universal. For example, sexual contact with a patient is universally prohibited, and is not supported by any theoretical or atheoretical approach. Maintaining patient confidentiality is another ethical standard that has even been codified into legal statutes in the United States. There are a variety of other ethical considerations that are universally accepted. None of these have been raised as criticisms of the Ericksonian approach.

Erickson was quite aware of a number of concerns about possible detrimental effects and potential abuses of hypnosis, especially in regard to untoward manipulation. As an expression of his strong personal ethical standards, he investigated these concerns. In 1932 Erickson published an article in the *Journal of Abnormal and Social Psychology*, in which he reviewed all available literature on the deleterious effects of hypnosis. Concerns at that time posited that hypnosis resulted in the enslavement of the personality, destruction of the will power, and automatizing of the innocent subject. No empirical validation of any such charges could be found by Erickson in the scientific literature of the day. He also examined concerns that individuals who were hypnotized might develop problems such as hypersuggestibility, personality alteration, loss of the ability to differentiate between reality and fantasy, and unhealthy mental attitudes or escape mechanisms. His sample group was his own work with approximately 300 different subjects, some of whom had been hypnotized more than 500 times each during a period of 4 to 6 years. He could find no cases which substantiated these concerns.

It also was commonly feared that hypnotized individuals could be induced or coerced into behaving in ways that were either anti-social or at odds with their own values. Erickson (1939) published a controlled study that compared subject behaviour in the normal waking and hypnotic states. These subjects were given tasks that were unethical or in violation of their own desires. In all cases they declined to comply in the hypnotic state. In some instances they demonstrated greater compliance in the waking state, and they were more expressive of irritation at the untoward demands in the hypnotic state. Erickson concluded that hypnosis cannot be misused to induce hypnotized persons to commit wrongful acts against themselves or others.

Manipulative

The criticism that Ericksonian psychotherapy is manipulative, stems to some degree from issues surrounding informed consent. The Ericksonian approach emphasizes communication on multiple levels, and utilizes the unconscious mind in mobilizing resources. Implicit in these methods is a therapeutic impact beyond conscious awareness. How, then, can one give informed consent, when, in fact, it is conscious awareness that must be 'informed'?

This is a complex issue which is aggravated by a conflict implicit in the treatment process. The conflict stems from the fact that the patient is seeking a change that he or she, for whatever reason, is unable to consciously effect independently. In the case of many Ericksonian interventions which mobilize unconscious resources, obtaining informed consent might well render the intervention ineffective. For example, John might like to assert himself and move out of the house to start college, but long-standing awareness of his parents' aversive reactions may prevent him from taking that step. A direct approach suggesting that he stand up to his parents might conjure up visions of prior confrontations resulting in a direct refusal. However, a well placed historical metaphor (especially if John were a patriot, or a revolutionary war buff) about America moving away from King George, the consequent conflict, and the ultimate alliance and respect now enjoyed by the two nations, might have a very different result. In that example, informed consent would involve explicitly telling John that the technique of multilevel metaphors would be employed to influence his behaviour, resulting in a new way of thinking about his situation, so that in the end, he would do what he was ambivalent about doing, and stand up to his parents. John might give permission, but the effectiveness of the metaphoric intervention could be seriously compromised.

Is metaphor manipulative? Decidedly. The posited intervention deliberately reframes John's choice so that it is something different from a simple disagreement with his parents. It also gives him an opportunity to make a choice that he might otherwise have seen as impossibly stressful. In practical terms, manipulation is exactly what John came to therapy to get. Before he came to treatment, John was aware of his conflicting desires for family peace and personal growth. It is axiomatic that John, and every other voluntary patient, has already experienced that internal stalemate (resistance to change) and consciously elected to seek treatment in order to somehow break the deadlock. Treatment that merely informs him that he can continue to suffer at home or face the conflict is no treatment at all.

In medical practice, where the concept of consent to treatment originated, the dynamics are very different. A patient seeks assistance, for example, because he is unable to remedy his chest pains. His diagnosis and the recommended procedure (open heart surgery) are explained to him, along with the potential benefits and risks. It is posited that the patient's full understanding of the procedure should not radically change the effectiveness of the procedure, should the patient elect to proceed.

Detailed procedural consent in the psychotherapeutic domain may, in at least some instances, be contraindicated. There is a distinction between conscious awareness, and what might be termed 'self-conscious' awareness, which goes beyond simple experience of the intervention, to observation of self throughout the intervention process. Using the previous example of John, conscious awareness following (uninformed) presentation of the metaphor might be experienced as a realization of a sense of empowerment and broader understanding of the cost/benefit ratio of confronting the conflict with parents. Negative 'self-conscious' (informed) awareness following the same intervention might be experienced as 'So I'm supposed to think of myself as George Washington or something? That was no big deal for him, he HAD a job and a place to stay, and a wife that was supportive of his decisions. How does that help me face Mom and Dad?' It requires therapist discretion to decide when the patient is well advised to have 'self-conscious' awareness.

Different approaches may benefit from 'self-conscious' awareness secondary to full procedural explanation. For instance, Eye Movement Desensitization and Reprocessing (EMDR) provides the patient with a detailed description of the process and ways that they may be affected, so that the patient may be aware of internal experiences related to the intervention process in order to report to the clinician on an ongoing basis.

In summary, Ericksonian therapy has been characterized as manipulative – a valid critique. It is the position of the authors that all effective therapies are manipulative to some degree, and one is advised to see past the negative connotation generally attached to the term 'manipulation', and determine whether or not a given manipulation is beneficial. Even the Rogerian approach which is in many ways the least intrusive of approaches, delineates methods of reflective listening that are geared to draw the patient out (manipulate the patient into saying more). Rogerian manipulation, like various Ericksonian manipulations, is in service of assisting the patient, and is in fact what the patient is seeking from treatment.

Directive

Ericksonian therapy has been criticized because it is directive. This is a criticism that emanates from quarters where the patient sets the pace and direction of therapy. In Rogerian (client-centred) therapy, the patient is encouraged to talk about his feelings in a context where the therapist responds with unconditional positive regard, genuineness and empathy. Beyond that, the therapist is encouraged to be personally as unobtrusive as possible. The theory holds that these conditions will foster the development of self-discovery and consequent growth. Similarly, in the psychodynamic approach, the therapist is meant to be a shadowy (non-descript) figure so as to facilitate the process of transference, which is the projection of the patient's inner conflicts onto the analyst/patient relationship. In both these approaches, giving directives would disrupt the process and, indeed, constitute a procedural, and perhaps even ethical, violation.

Other approaches are quite directive, and could not be effective if they weren't. Rational Emotive Behaviour Therapy routinely uses behavioural assignments to either initiate or ratify change. It is clear that the merits of giving directives are relative to the therapeutic approach in question.

Yapko has written cogently about concerns related to a directive Ericksonian psychotherapy:

> Critics often argue that the [directive] approach is manipulative – that is, clients are treated as if dehumanized chess pieces to be moved about on the therapist's game board. Critics further argue that the practice of directive therapy may be unethical because the client is not fully informed as to either the reasons for, or the expected outcomes, of treatment strategies (thus precluding a truly informed consent to treatment).
>
> In fact, when directive approaches to therapy are used appropriately, they revolve so completely around the client's needs and abilities that no more person-centered approach seems possible. . . . It is the clients who choose the goal, and it is the clients who are fully accepted in terms of their personal frame of reference. Furthermore, the client is the controlling force in what does and doesn't get carried out in therapy – just as in almost every other therapeutic modality. The main advantage of directive techniques is the emphasis on *experiential learning* – the acknowledgment that the most significant and memorable learnings occur in real-life contexts. (Yapko, 1990: 380)

Critics of directive approaches or techniques are not only concerned that self-referential growth processes are disrupted by intrusive direction, but there is a concern that the therapist might impose his or her own values on a vulnerable patient. In Chapter 2 we quoted Erickson about rendering his opinion to patients – he wondered why he should sit by and allow someone to potentially ruin his life, and not say a word. And he gave several examples where he had given directives and opinions. We chose to quote him verbatim there because his words reflect a caring for his patients (not a caring for his opinion), and a respect that recognizes his patient's autonomy and ability to hear an opinion or directive, and make his or her own decision as to how to proceed.

Ericksonian therapy is often directive. Those directives, when followed, provide patients with an experience that can impact not only their presenting complaint, but that also can alter self-perception in ways that permit systemic change. The notion that any directive approach is problematic is simply invalid.

Superficial
The Ericksonian approach has been characterized as superficial, owing to its brief nature and focus on symptom relief rather than the development of insight. As with other criticisms reviewed here, it is acknowledged that treatment is indeed brief in most cases, and that this approach does pursue problem resolution without regard for insight development. One must evaluate whether or not these facts speak to a genuine inadequacy of the approach (decrement in patient care), in assessing whether or not the claim of superficiality is valid.

Yapko (1990) wrote about the issue of superficiality. He was discussing brief and directive approaches which:

. . . [have] the ability to address underlying dynamics through experiential learning rather than through insight. Such learnings are more multidimensional and are less prone to be restricted to new intellectual understandings only. While critics often dislike the emphasis on solutions and outcomes instead of on the growth process, they often fail to recognize that growth involves progressively developing new solutions to old problems. (Yapko, 1990: 380–1)

Zeig also addressed the charge that Ericksonian therapy is superficial at the expense of insight:

. . . as Ericksonian therapists work with a symptom, they expect a snowballing effect. Gaining competence over a symptom breaks patients out of rigid mind sets. Subsequently there can be salutary reverberations into other aspects of the patient's life, including the patient's social system. . . .Psychological insight has been viewed [from other perspectives] as antithetical to the Ericksonian approach, which is seen as directed to stimulating the patient's unconscious and bypassing conscious understandings. Actually, insight can be used within Ericksonian methodologies: It is merely one of a number of health promoting methods. If insight could be used to catalyze change, Erickson utilized it. More often, however, understanding *why* does not help people discover *how* to do things differently. . . . Change is independent of insight. (Zeig, 1990b: 375–6)

With regard to insight, Lankton (1990) concurs: 'It is from the learning brought by new actions and not from insight or understanding that change develops' (p. 365).

The charge that Ericksonian therapy is superficial is erroneous. Noted practitioners of this method affirm that strategic interventions have the effect of disrupting ingrained dysfunctional patterns, consequently inducing second-order change that often can be quite dramatic. For example, Erickson (1960) told of a woman who weighed 240 pounds and had tried and failed at diets over the course of several years. During hypnosis he gave her the suggestion that she should follow the diet her doctor had prescribed, and that when she sat down to eat she would experience time distortion in such a way that meals would seem to her to last for hours. She returned nine months after that single session weighing 120 pounds to report that time distortion had worked, and she was more satisfied with her social and recreational activities as well. Brief treatment. No insight. Systemic improvement.

As a final note in reference to the notion that Erickson's work or approach was unethical, either by commission or omission, we would like to state emphatically that the idea is entirely unsupported. No universally applied ethical standards are even remotely violated. This approach unabashedly deviates from guidelines that are applicable to other approaches, but those are guidelines essential and applicable only to the theoretical underpinnings and technical mechanisms of those approaches.

Personal Criticisms

Although the next group of criticisms is not an attack on Erickson or his integrity, we have elected to label them as personal because the concerns stem more from who he was than from the work he did. Specifically, the criticisms are that he was a cult figure, and that as a charismatic individual, the work that he did cannot be done by others.

Those who have read Chapter 1 know that Erickson led an incredibly interesting life peppered with astonishing accomplishments, that he was a man with a playful sense of humour, that he was intensely interested in people and *their* lives, and that he was a pioneer driven by curiosity and talent. Taken as a whole, these traits indeed made him sought after as a teacher, consultant, mentor and therapist. The notoriety that ensued was an artifact of the knowledge he had to contribute, as opposed to a desire for fame. One can argue that indeed it was the accomplishments that attracted people, not the man; since his death, more than 10,000 practitioners have attended the six International Congresses on Ericksonian Methods of Psychotherapy alone. Moreover, Erickson was made 'famous' more by the writings of his students than by his personal efforts.

Cult

Certainly, in order to assess whether or not Erickson was a cult figure, we must define what that term means. Most cult figures are charismatic, have a philosophy or set of beliefs they promote (and to which they demand their followers adhere), encourage loyalty in their followers even above family, and participate in active recruitment of followers.

Erickson seems to fit the first two characteristics in that he was charismatic and he was willing to teach those who came to him to learn. That personal appeal, however, may not be central to the development of his following. One of the authors of this text (Munion) never met the man, yet is very interested in his intellectual legacy, and therapeutic concepts cannot be characterized as 'charismatic'. The likely explanation is that Erickson was a charismatic man with a compelling approach to psychotherapy.

Erickson did provide countless lectures, demonstrations, papers, chapters and co-authored books about his ideas. Therefore, the notion that he promoted his philosophy and beliefs is valid. But implicit in his ideas was that the individual patient was always to be met within his personal frame of reference. Erickson's teaching style was the polar opposite of dogmatic, and scholars are unable to come up with any manifesto that he originated. Aside from encouraging that his students attended to who their patients were and to the resources they bring to the therapeutic encounter, Erickson appeared to be disinterested in whether or not others elected to proceed as he would.

There is no indication that Erickson demanded loyalty from his students or patients. He promoted family values and did family therapy when the practice was unheard of among psychiatrists. While it may be true that, given the right circumstances, he might help someone who was being victimized in an abusive relationship to realize that they had alternatives, it was not his way to make life choices for his patients.

In response to the question of whether or not Erickson sought followers, Zeig, who *did* know Erickson, wrote, 'Erickson was a firm believer in the importance of individuality, and he would not have appreciated imitation. He preferred that people develop their own unique styles' (Zeig, 1990b: 375).

Was Erickson a cult figure? No more so than any other founder of a major approach to psychotherapy. Any teacher or impactful innovator naturally has followers. Cult (at least in the pejorative sense of the word) doesn't seem to emanate from charisma or teachings or belief systems, but from whether or not those components are misused.

Not Everyone Can Do What He Did

It is tempting to encapsulate the whole of this section into the single word 'true' and leave it at that. The stated criticism is that his charismatic nature allowed him to be effective in ways that others could not be. Erickson would probably agree, but not necessarily because he believed himself to be charismatic. Likely he would agree because he recognized that his particular combination of talents and weaknesses were unlike anyone else's. Therefore, it was obvious that no one could be effective in the same ways as he. For instance, if he were asked to assist someone in improving their self-confidence, he would not have demonstrated crossing a rope bridge, climbing a rock face, and rapelling down a cliff, and then assisted the patient in doing these activities. Such adventure-based programmes exist, and participants do report that participation can be a transforming process. Erickson, however, was wheelchair-bound for a significant portion of his later life. He, therefore, would have found another way, a different way, which not only utilized his patient's resources, but complimented his own therapeutic strengths as well. He prized individuality so much, and his therapy was so oriented to the unique assets of each patient, that no one can question that he expected each therapist would naturally do therapy in a unique way.

Perhaps more to the point is the question of whether or not those characteristics that made him charismatic, (a) could be learnt by any therapist and (b) were fundamental to his approach. We touched on charisma to some degree in the previous section. Erickson's life was a collection of interesting experiences and accomplishments; he was a man with a playful sense of humour; he was intensely interested in people and *their* lives; and he was a pioneer driven by curiosity and talent.

Experiences, accomplishments and talent are not easily acquired, but they do make a person interesting, which is probably a significant component of charisma. Playfulness was also a very appealing aspect of Erickson, and it came naturally. But what really makes one interesting and appealing is to be *interested*, to have a genuine 'other' focus, with no elements of self-absorption. The authors suggest that, in terms of personal attributes, if the therapist is genuinely interested in the patient and his or her life, then the therapist will be sufficiently 'charismatic' in order to do Ericksonian psychotherapy.

As to whether or not Erickson's personal appeal to others was essential to his therapeutic effectiveness, we can say for certain that that was not always the case. There are well-documented cases where Erickson was deliberately abrasive or abrupt with patients. Oddly this seemed to be an effective approach in the particular cases described – which only serves to underscore once again the importance of careful observation and willingness to meet patients in their particular frames of reference.

If attendance at conferences and training is a valid indicator of how many therapists are incorporating elements of the Ericksonian approach into their therapy, then there is substantial evidence that a great many people can, to some degree, do what Erickson did. In fact, any therapist who approaches the therapy process prepared to treat each patient as an individual, and to tailor treatment to fit patient resources and needs, has already gone a long way towards doing *exactly* what Erickson could do; the remainder is acquiring suitable technical skills.

Yes, some of the aforementioned reasoning is polemic and overstated. Not everyone can do what Erickson did. Erickson was a genius, of that there is no doubt. Only a rare few possess genius. None of Erickson's students have been able to fully replicate his effectiveness, even at simply inducing hypnosis. However, the authors do not want the label 'genius' to be used as an epithet that frightens novices away. In many ways, genius is attention to detail, combined with creativity. If we merely dismiss Erickson as a singular genius, we may lose the opportunity to develop our own creativity and attention to detail.

Approach Limitations

It has been suggested that Erickson's approach is only applicable to a limited population or variety of problems. It has also been suggested that the therapist needs a lot of patients in order to make a living. Each of these criticisms requires that the available literature be given merely a cursory examination in order to determine its validity.

Applicability
Some critics have charged that Erickson's approach has limited application; that it is only effective with certain patient populations.

Perhaps the simplest means of verifying this concern is to examine O'Hanlon and Hexum's (1990) *An Uncommon Casebook*, which reviews and summarizes Erickson's case studies. They found that Erickson added more cases to the literature than any other therapist in history. The book divides the case studies into the following groups – Habits and Compulsions; Physical Problems and Pain; Sexual Problems; Sleep Problems; Phobias and Emotional Problems; Cognitive and Communication Problems; Marital, Family and Relationship Problems; Severe Disturbances of Behaviour and Cognition; and other Miscellaneous Problems. Given this range of problems, it is difficult to imagine an approach that is any more *broadly* applicable.

Perhaps the individuals who have concerns about applicability are thinking strictly in terms of populations that can and will sit placidly in a chair to be passively cured through direct suggestion delivered during formal trance induction. That group of patients may indeed be fairly small, but Erickson's work was clearly not limited to either that population or that approach. While he was cautious to keep medical problems separate from psychological problems, he was willing to meet virtually any sort of psychological presenting complaint within the patient's frame of reference. Formal hypnosis was not required in a large percentage of cases.

Since Erickson was willing to utilize any aspect of patient functioning in creating interventions, he had a flexibility that permitted him to treat populations in ways that other approaches could not. Classical psychoanalysis cannot be done briefly and is seldom available to indigent individuals. Cognitive approaches are challenged in working with mentally retarded patients. Behavioural approaches are of little assistance in helping a couple to work through a marital affair. In short, while formal trance induction may be inappropriate in many cases, Erickson's approach was much more than hypnosis – it was, in fact, nearly universally applicable.

Making a Living

It has been suggested that anyone competent in Ericksonian psychotherapy will need a lot of patients in order to earn a living. This particular criticism must be regarded as somewhat 'tongue in cheek', and speaks to the notion that, since Ericksonian interventions are often rapidly effective, patients come and go quickly, and any given patient is likely to be a small source of revenue. What could be better? Few in the helping professions doubt that there is more than enough pain and suffering to keep us all busy for years to come.

An examination of the literature indicates that many of Erickson's interventions were limited to a few sessions, or even just one. That same literature review reveals that a substantial number of patients returned intermittently for months and even years. Each patient's needs determined the duration of treatment.

It should be noted that (in the same 'tongue in cheek' vein), if Erickson shot himself in the foot by curing patients quickly, he shot himself in the other foot by providing service to individuals who could not afford it, either for free, or sometimes in exchange for performance for some service around his home or office. This type of exchange allowed the patient to have a sense of participation and dignity, and required an investment that probably enhanced treatment effects.[1] Erickson made it known that he was interested in people's lives, not their money.

Such exchange was not limited to patients. In *Taproots*, O'Hanlon (1987) explained how it was that he came to meet and learn from Erickson. As it turns out, O'Hanlon was a student who was doing some gardening as a means of augmenting his finances. Erickson took him up on his offer to weed gardens in exchange for instruction. Not all of Erickson's students paid or worked it off. Jeffrey Zeig was Erickson's student for more than six years. He did not have the funds to pay Erickson, and was never charged. He did, however, return the moral obligation to Erickson by seeing patients who could not afford treatment, and by establishing The Milton H. Erickson Foundation.

Here again, Erickson met his student within his particular frame of reference. If it was important enough in the student's value system to offer to work, then Erickson honoured that value with opportunity.

Conclusion

We have reviewed a number of criticisms of the Ericksonian approach to psychotherapy. Our depth assessment of these critiques is that in many cases there is some validity to the criticism, but often only from a narrow perspective. Those criticisms that are secondary to the atheoretical nature of the approach, have some validity, but fail to recognize the value that is gained on the patient's behalf where the benefits of theoretical structure are relinquished. The criticisms that question the ethics of this approach do so from a parochial perspective which assumes that components or values necessary to one approach are necessary to all. The criticisms that focus on Erickson's personal characteristics in essence look at the degree to which anyone but Erickson can do Ericksonian psychotherapy. These are valid to the degree that each therapist is unique, but any therapist so inspired can join their patients in their personal frame of reference in search of a solution that is unique and derived from the patients' personal resources. Finally, the criticisms relevant to range of applicability and absolute treatment duration appear to be founded strictly in conjecture – they are false or spurious.

Note

1. Bartering is generally unethical in current American Psychological Association ethics.

5

The Overall Influence of Milton H. Erickson

> . . . whenever you deal with patients, you deal with them not only
> in terms of the immediate present but also in terms of future
> perspectives and possibilities.
>
> Milton H. Erickson (Rossi and Ryan, 1985: 7)

The purpose of Chapter 5 is to examine Erickson's profound impact
on the contemporary practice of psychotherapy. His efforts fostered
the following changes in the field:

1. Clinical hypnosis has become a legitimate and respected treatment approach;
2. there has been a focal shift away from insight/understanding to
   demonstrable change, and a concomitant shift in orientation
   from the past to the present and future;
3. short-term and solution-focused methods have gained increased
   acceptance and utilization;
4. humour and drama have gained respect within the domain of
   legitimate psychotherapeutic and hypnotic interventions;
5. there is an increased attention to using the context within which
   human functioning occurs;
6. Erickson's work has developed a worldwide following;
7. Erickson's work has spawned several derivative schools.

An underlying factor accounting for Erickson's broad impact was
his empirical investigations of the hypnotic phenomena with which
he worked. Erickson's interest in research lent credence to his work
in a climate that was not especially receptive to some aspects of his
approach.

Rejection of Erickson's work commonly stemmed from two
issues: its atheoretical (or anti-theoretical) nature, and the fact that
much of his work was in the field of hypnosis, which was summarily
dismissed by Freud.

Erickson eschewed theories because they limit the way in which
practitioners view the patient and the problem. Many of Erickson's
interventions ran counter to the theoretical postulates of major

schools of therapy (for example, Erickson was directive, which is antithetical to psychodynamic and client-centred approaches). Restated succinctly, Erickson viewed the patient and problem, without the limitations imposed by theory, with an eye for the resources and abilities available to the patient, which he utilized to assist the patient in problem resolution through a variety of innovative methods. The interventions he effected were often unique, elegant, powerful and deceptively simple. These qualities have led to Erickson's popularity as evidenced by the proliferation of books, conferences and trainings about his approaches. Also, a number of derivative schools are based on Erickson's work. All of these approaches are steeped in the principle of parsimony. Focusing on essential elements of change and eliminating non-essentials assured that his approach was practical.

Parsimony in Erickson's Approach

Erickson demonstrated that understanding was not a precondition of change. In order to ride a bicycle, you do not need to know physics. So too, individuals can achieve behavioural change without developing insight into the unconscious forces that may have determined the behaviour. Erickson observed people, their resources, abilities, life situation and their problems. He devised ways to assist them in reconfiguring internal life and social situations so that change became inevitable and was effected to the patients' credit. In the process, he challenged the theories of other approaches, much as he challenged his grandfather's superstition that potatoes should be planted with eyes up during a specific phase of the moon (see Chapter 1). If Erickson wanted to grow potatoes he certainly would have dug a hole and covered each potato piece with earth and water, but he would have dispensed with the unnecessary portions of his grandfather's procedures.

Erickson had a gift for perceiving not only what comprised the essential elements of change, but also for ascertaining when an approach was essential with one individual, but irrelevant with another. For example, in Chapter 2, we contrasted the case of Inhibited Ann with that of another couple. With Ann, Erickson exercised restraint due to his concern for Ann's modesty (he was almost Rogerian in that regard), but his approach with the second couple was decidedly unrestrained. He recognized that the couple could profit from a directive that was shocking and even coarse ('. . . why in hell don't you fuck for fun and pray to the devil that she isn't knocked up for at least three months', Rossi *et al.*, 1983: 205). In this second case he sensed that concern for the couple's sense of modesty was irrelevant, and that a graphic approach would be more effective.

In the 1940s, it was virtually unheard of for a psychiatrist to do family therapy, but Erickson did it in some circumstances because it made sense and facilitated the therapy process. It was not that Erickson decided to invent family therapy. Rather, he was interested in expediting change. If seeing family would facilitate change, that was what he did in his practice.

Subsequently, we are confronted with the dilemma of assessing Erickson's impact on the field of psychotherapy. One cannot credit him with establishing family therapy yet he stepped into that arena before there *was* such an arena, and his strategic family interventions are still influential today – for example, through the work of Haley, Madanes and Stephen and Carol Lankton.

Other schools (psychodynamic, affective, behavioural, cognitive, relational, etc.) address select aspects of individual functioning – Erickson addressed real individuals in all facets of their functioning. Therefore, we can see aspects of all the aforementioned schools in his work. And, conversely many schools include Erickson's methods in their approach. Hence the line is blurred – Erickson was not a family therapist, but he worked with families; he was not a behaviourist, but he worked with behaviours (and behaviourally). Similarly, for example, the fact that some cognitive approaches incorporate Erickson's methods does not make them 'Ericksonian'.

As someone who worked in all aspects of human functioning, Erickson's impact was not directed toward the establishment of a distinct school. He was decidedly against a separate school of 'Ericksonian Therapy'. Rather, his impact was found in innovations that bear his personal stamp. In the remaining portion of this chapter we will examine the major impact of his work in the field of psychotherapy, with an eye toward what was uniquely Erickson in those domains. One of Erickson's singular contributions was in the field of hypnosis.

Hypnotherapy

Owing to its rejection by Freud, hypnosis was viewed with disfavour early in the twentieth century, and is viewed, even today (by the uninformed), with apprehension. As discussed in Chapter 4, Erickson dispelled the common myths about hypnosis. In the course of his research and practice, Erickson transformed hypnosis from a phenomena targeted for academic inquiry (and occasional show business exploitation) into a legitimate and powerfully effective treatment tool. Chapter 3 reviewed a number of hypnotic developments, and a variety of strategic technical innovations that Erickson effected.

The nature and extent of Erickson's impact on the practice of clinical hypnosis defies measurement. Erickson was the dominant figure in the field of twentieth-century hypnosis. To be sure, before Erickson there was hypnosis, and there were individuals who sought to use hypnosis to relieve psychological distress. Traditional hypnosis was, however, mechanistic at best, and far more focused on trance development and the use of protocols for therapy. It was not a flexible patient-oriented approach. Erickson devised ways to skilfully interweave therapy into the trance induction and experience. He took principles from hypnosis and applied them to therapy without the necessity of relying on formal trances.

Erickson's contributions to hypnosis were widely recognized. Academic researchers, including Irving Kirsch, Steven Jay Lynn and Judith W. Rhue (1993) discussed Erickson and his work as one of the historical milestones in the history of hypnosis, indicating he advanced the use and acceptability of hypnosis in clinical practice. In a similar vein, clinicians such as Bernie Zilbergeld, M. Gerald Edelstein and Daniel L. Araoz (1986) characterized Milton Erickson as a master therapist and a masterful hypnotist, indicating that he was the person largely responsible for the renewed interest in hypnosis.

As is often the case with Erickson's therapy, it is not one thing or another at work, it is one thing *and* another at work. This is true when it comes to examining Erickson's impact on the practice of hypnotherapy as well. One thing at work was the long arduous hours of research that simultaneously taught Erickson so much about hypnosis, and established his reputation as a thoughtful scientist and skilful observer. Another thing at work was Erickson's innovative approaches to treatment, which were integrated with hypnosis to produce dramatically effective results. The combination of his scientific credibility and his therapeutic efficacy accounted for Erickson being credited with advancing the cause of hypnotherapy.

All of the leading figures in hypnosis reacted to Erickson's work. One of his commentators was André Weitzenhoffer. Weitzenhoffer (1989), who contributed significantly to the practice, theory and research of clinical hypnosis, wrote about hypnotism, and struggled with the issue of defining Erickson's role in its development. Ultimately, he distinguished traditional and semi-traditional approaches from the Ericksonian approach, which he labelled as non-traditional. He recognized traditional and semi-traditional approaches as hypnotist centred, and the Ericksonian approach as client centred, deriving the intervention from within the patient. He stopped short, however, of proclaiming the Ericksonian approach as superior. Weitzenhoffer stated that there were elements of the Ericksonian approach in semi-traditional hypnotism, which is an adaptation of traditional hypnotherapy that 'gives special attention to the contributions the subject can make to the overall process' (1989: 1). Weitzenhoffer (1989) identified utilization as the hallmark of the Ericksonian approach, and acknowledged that Erickson was probably the first to explicitly recognize and methodically develop that process (1989: 191).

Demonstration

Weitzenhoffer (1989) recounted watching Erickson perform a demonstration that epitomized the therapeutic style that Erickson pioneered. It is an example of Erickson's non-traditional style of hypnosis and his faith in the indirect method that he pioneered. During this particular demonstration, the subject developed a good trance, but failed to manifest the desired trance phenomena. Erickson continued to engage her in a conversational tone and casually picked up a piece of paper which he rolled into a cylinder. He apparently absent-mindedly let the paper tube unfurl once, rolled it up again, then pointed it once at his subject, stuck his finger into the tube, withdrew it and then let it unroll and fall to the floor in disinterest. After that point, the subject responded quite well by developing all requested trance phenomena.

Weitzenhoffer later questioned Erickson about the incident and learned what had happened. During the demonstration, Erickson realized that he had encountered and worked with this female subject a year earlier, and that she had worn an engagement ring at that time. Since she presently wore neither engagement nor wedding ring, Erickson surmised that her resistance was a result of fear that her failed engagement would be at issue during the demonstration. He had non-verbally conveyed to her a disinterest in that subject, and the demonstration was able to proceed apace. This incident is an excellent example of Erickson's ability to look at the situation in minute detail, and then to communicate either to the conscious or unconscious mind in a way that resolves resistances and solves a problem.

There appears to be good reason to assert that Erickson's work significantly advanced the clinical practice of hypnosis. He pioneered methods of hypnotherapy that utilize and integrate the patient's strengths and abilities. He contributed a substantial research base that expanded the understanding of hypnosis and hypnotic phenomena, and in the process developed new hypnotic techniques. He was instrumental in the founding and developing of major hypnosis organizations such as the American Society of

Clinical Hypnosis and its journal, *The American Journal of Clinical Hypnosis*, which he edited for the first 10 years following its inception. And, his published successes stimulated the interest of practitioners seeking effective therapeutic interventions.

The Constructive Unconscious

Erickson developed a positive perspective of the unconscious, which was a basis for the advancements that he made in the practice of hypnotherapy. He saw it as a powerful resource for change, as well as a font of information and abilities. He looked at the unconscious mind as something more than an 'unseen' determinant of pathological behaviour, as it was regarded in the psychoanalytic tradition. More importantly, he realized that since the unconscious was a behavioural determinant that was outside of awareness, it could be used to elicit positive behavioural/functional change, without the development of insight. Indirect suggestions would elicit unconscious processes, circumvent resistance and create new and positive experiences for the patient.

A second way that Erickson impacted the field of psychotherapy was that he pioneered a practical, future-oriented method.

Focal Shift

This view of the unconscious as a constructive change agent was truly profound, and impacted Erickson's treatment approach enormously even where hypnosis was not involved. Since many other approaches had little or no overt interest in the unconscious mind as an agent of change (for example, insight development is a conscious phenomenon), Erickson's vision of the unconscious mind did not impact on these approaches. The *implication* of his vision, however, was far reaching. One of the foundations of Erickson's work is the notion that unconscious therapeutic change is possible and often desirable. Once insight development is eliminated as a fundamental requirement for therapeutic change, interventions of all sorts become possible. Brief, strategic, solution-focused and systems-oriented interventions all have their roots in this paradigm shift, and Erickson's work was seminal in the development of these innovations. Similarly, other approaches (e.g. cognitive-behavioural) have profited from the validation generated by the array of successful interventions that disregard insight development in favour of functional change.

At first blush, a concept that focuses on creating functional change bears a resemblance to behavioural (learning-theory driven) approaches. Erickson, however, differed from behavioural approaches methodologically. For example, it was common for him to successfully work through a problem symbolically, because the patient was not ready to deal with issues consciously. To this end, he used metaphors, anecdotes or even ambiguous function assignments (for information about ambiguous function assignments, see Lankton and Lankton, 1983). While the focus or outcome of such 'non-congruent' approaches might be functional change, there is nothing technically 'behavioural' in such interventions.

A second impact of moving away from insight development is the ability to focus therapeutically on the future instead of the past. A review of Erickson's cases shows a teleological orientation. Of course, there was recognition of the role of the past in fostering the patient's present dilemma, but Erickson's focus was consistently on how the future would be with the problem resolved. Whereas insight-oriented therapies describe the past, leading to an understanding of aetiology, in contrast, a future-oriented approach describes the problem in the present and looks toward the nature of desired and possible and inevitable change. One cannot change an unchangeable past. One can ensure a constructive future.

One of the ways in which Erickson created a future orientation, and at the same time utilized the unconscious mind, was to hypnotically induce patients to develop a vision of their future, at a time when their particular problem had been resolved. This technique (future projection) is illustrated in the case description that follows:

Crystal Balls   A female patient reached an impasse in her treatment with Erickson (1954b and Rossi, 1980d). She experienced anxiety, depression, withdrawal, and dependency. She also narrowed her focus in therapy to an intellectual rehashing of her problems. In spite of her dislike of living with her parents, she resisted opportunities to move out. She bitterly complained about her job, but refused to apply for an available promotion. She wanted and needed social contact, but avoided chances to engage. Although she initially had a positive response to hypnosis, she had become increasingly resistive and negative.

At one point, she emphasized repeatedly that she felt that if she could achieve even one of her goals, the rest would surely follow. Erickson seized on that opportunity and instructed the patient, in a hypnotic state, to hallucinate a series of crystal balls in which significant events in her life would be depicted. Out of these images, her unconscious mind would divine a meaningful pattern which would help to formulate an image of her future, depicted in a separate crystal ball, in which she was engaged pleasantly and happily in some activity. The patient did all of this, finding herself fascinated with the future scene. She saw herself at a friend's wedding, which was still some three months in the future. In that vision, she wore a beautiful dress, danced with several men, and even accepted a date with one of the wedding guests. She told Erickson all about her hallucination. He concluded trance with instructions for amnesia for the trance experience.

The patient returned to therapy twice more during the next few weeks, and on both occasions, asked for hypnosis. In trance, she stated that she should be told to re-experience all she had seen and felt unconsciously during the hallucinated wedding scene. She then discontinued therapy. Several days after the wedding she entered Erickson's office and reported all that had transpired as anticipated since the last session. She had become so involved in her friend's wedding that she had been invited to become a bridesmaid. To facilitate these efforts, she had moved to an apartment in town in order to eliminate three hours of travel time between her parent's home and work. Since she made her own dress and therefore needed more money, she applied for, and got, a promotion at work. She arranged bridal showers for her friend. At the wedding, she had struck up a relationship and dated one of the guests (though not the guest she had envisioned). She thanked Erickson for helping her to feel better, without realizing that it was her preparations for the wedding, her vision, which had resolved her problems.

Erickson's focus on future comes at least in part from observations of hypnotic subjects who demonstrated the ability to become fully immersed in the experience of age regression. Erickson reasoned that if subjects could vividly re-experience past events in their lives, and even incorporate hypnotically induced memories as 'real' events, then hypnotically experienced futures could have an equally 'real' impact. His work with age progression led to the understanding that a trance was not a prerequisite to developing a future orientation. Non-hypnotic therapy could orient to the future, and a future orientation is common among many therapeutic approaches today. It has been adopted into the therapeutic culture through the work of Steve de Shazer and his associates who developed the solution-focused approach. Erickson pioneered efforts to develop a vision of a healthy future as a foundation of therapy.

A third major contribution of Erickson, was his pioneering work in brief therapy.

Short-term/Solution-focused Approaches

Since insight was not a critical outcome for successful treatment in Erickson's view, interventions could be solution-focused and treatment duration could be brief. Short-term/solution-focused methods have gained increased acceptance and utilization as a result of his work.

An extraordinary number of Erickson's cases consisted of one or a few therapeutic contacts. At the time when Erickson began practising, the established major approaches (psychodynamic, client centred, behavioural) required multiple sessions at best, and often years of treatment with multiple sessions weekly. Erickson's brief approach was a radical departure, and he is one of the founding fathers of the brief treatment movement. His approach was predicated on the respectful belief that patients, given minimal assistance in overcoming an immediate difficulty, are best qualified to manage their own lives and problems. Moreover, as Jay Haley indicated, therapy is a problem, not a solution. The problem is that the patient is in therapy. The solution is to get the patient out of therapy, living life independent of therapy as quickly as possible.

We have previously reviewed a number of his short-term successes. The African Violet Queen of Milwaukee was a fine example of single session intervention. The business woman who was fearful of flying and had to go to Dallas was able to fly comfortably after one session, and lost her fear of suspension bridges as well after two. The literature on Erickson abounds with such cases.

Few sessions, however, did not always mean short ones. In a conversation with Jay Haley (Haley, 1985a), Erickson recounted treating a woman psychiatrist who wanted desperately to establish social relations. The woman was about to move to another city, and would be leaving her only two friends behind. Her hygiene was atrocious, consisting of greasy hair and filthy finger nails. She was consistently unbathed. Her clothing was mismatched, and she wore no makeup. Following an initial session during which he informed her that in order for therapy to succeed she would need to be totally compliant, he sent her home for three days to contemplate her level of commitment. The patient returned prepared to follow all instructions.

Erickson proceeded to review all of her grooming deficits in elaborate detail during the course of the next three hours, ultimately requiring her to wash half of her grimy neck in session in order to contrast the clean and dirty parts. She arrived for the next session clean, but without make up and wearing mismatched clothing. The details and progress from the previous session were reviewed. Erickson then told her that there was a fact that she had been ignoring that was apparent to everyone with whom she came in contact, and that he would give her a task that would make it impossible for her to ever forget it. As she left the second session, he instructed her to go home, stand nude in front of the mirror, and contemplate her 'three badges of womanhood'.

When she arrived for her third session, she was instructed in detail how to go about spending the US$700 she had set aside for therapy – she was to get a makeup and clothing consultation at a local department store; she was to purchase cloth, seek assistance, and make a gown to wear to a dance sponsored by her employers that was to take place a few weeks later; she was to obtain dance lessons; and she was to stop by to see Erickson on her way to that dance. She arrived on her way to the dance, as scheduled, well-groomed and had even lost some weight. Three months later she had begun her new position in another city, and she met a professor whom she married within the year. Erickson's therapeutic contacts were four sessions, if one counts the evening when she stopped by to see him on her way to the dance. And to be clear about it, Erickson would count that visit as very important, because she had given a commitment, and the visit to him virtually assured her attendance at the dance. The duration of the second session was three hours in this case. Protracted sessions such as this were not uncommon, and no doubt contributed significantly to Erickson's ability to create substantial therapeutic change in a relatively few number of visits. Therapy was extended to meet the demands of the moment and needs of the patient, not to address the convenience of the therapist.

Proliferation

Erickson pioneered brief, solution-focused work (Furman and Ahola, 1994), which led to a proliferation of such approaches within the field of psychotherapy. Notable among these are the strategic approach of Haley and Cloé Madanes, de Shazer's solution-focused approach as practised at the Brief Family Therapy Center in Milwaukee, and brief therapy as practised at the Mental Research Institute in Palo Alto. Again, these approaches are predicated on both a paradigm shift that prizes functional change in favour of insight development, and a belief in the patient's ability to profit from minimal intervention.

Humour and Drama

Erickson's approach was unfettered by theoretical constraints which would limit his range of interventions. For example, the theory-bound psychoanalyst, must strive to be neutral so that the patient will have a transference object. In contrast Erickson was at liberty to be himself, which meant that playfulness and humour were integrated into the therapy process. As a result, humour gained

respect within the domains of legitimate interventions, even within
formal trance.

Humour and drama were a natural part of Erickson's style. Both
of these means of communication lend themselves to carrying
pointed and memorable messages. Further, they are processed in a
non-linear way; that is, they are more experiential than cognitive.
Humour and drama capture the patient's full attention, and can
disrupt a problem-oriented frame of reference, allowing for a new
and therapeutic alternative to be considered, either consciously or
unconsciously. While drama is an excellent means of conveying new
ideas, humour has a positive balancing effect by inserting a gentle
reminder that life not only has its downs, but its ups as well.
Humour and drama can be considered independently. First, we will
examine Erickson's use of humour.

Humour

Erickson was a playful man, and this permeated his relations with
his family, friends, students and patients. Sidney Rosen reports that
Erickson once told him to 'spread humor knee deep everywhere'
(1988: 19). Cloé Madanes carried Erickson's perspective into her
work with families, noting:

> When people are irrationally grim, the introduction of playfulness can
> elicit new behavior and bring about new alternatives. A humorous
> redefinition, explanation, or directive takes the family by surprise in a
> way that gives strength, drama, and impact to the intervention. (1987:
> 51)

Erickson's use of humour could be straightforward or part of an
assignment. In one instance, he was treating a little girl who
behaved as if she were angry at everyone. It appears that she was
often teased about her copious freckles. When she met Erickson, she
appeared sullen and recalcitrant. As she stood glowering in the
doorway, he suddenly pointed at her and said, 'You're a thief! You
steal! . . . I even know what you stole. I even have proof that you
stole.' Her curiosity was aroused and she wanted to know what his
proof was. He told her that he knew she loved cinnamon biscuits
and that, one day when she was climbing up to get the biscuits from
the cookie jar, she spilled them on her face. The proof was the
cinnamon all over her face. She burst out laughing at his 'proof',
and they had a nice chat. His playful teasing had broken the
tension. After this, they carried on a correspondence and her bitterness subsided (Rosen, 1982: 152–4).

Recall his treatment of the disabled construction worker
described in the Metaphor section of Chapter 3. The assignment

given to the patient was to gather humorous articles and cartoons, and send them to injured co-workers to cheer them up. In the first case, Erickson made a joke as part of his intervention. In the second case, although Erickson made no effort at levity, humour was a fundamental part of the patient's assignment. Erickson also told jokes to patients while they were in trance. Hypnosis was not sacrosanct; the unconscious could be seen as responding to humour as well as more serious directives.

When William O'Hanlon (1987) approached Erickson about becoming a student, he wrote to Erickson that he had considered a number of ways of broaching the subject, one of which was to offer his services as a gardener. O'Hanlon was away the following weekend and when he returned, he learned that he had been getting phone calls from a mysterious man seeking O'Hanlon's Gardening Service. Sure enough, the calls were from Erickson.

It is not surprising, then, that O'Hanlon and his ex-wife, Patricia Hudson, have incorporated the use of humour into their therapy approach. They recommend developing creative and humorous behavioural alternatives in order to disrupt ingrained patterns. For example, a fellow who was told frequently by his wife during fights that she would castrate him, became somewhat immobilized by the comment. After considering alternatives with Pat, he elected to either squirt his wife with a water pistol, or hide under the kitchen table in mock fear when she made that comment. When he followed through, the argument was disrupted in a positive way (O'Hanlon and Hudson, 1994).

O'Hanlon underscored the value of using humour to introduce the unexpected and produce a therapeutic outcome. He recounted a case of Steve de Shazer, where parents were having a bad time with their teenage son, whom they characterized as belligerent, oppositional and disruptive. The selected intervention was to put all of the son's underwear in the freezer whenever he went out. When he looked for it, they would tell him it was in the freezer, and respond to his demands for explanation with a shrug of the shoulders. He began to behave somewhat more cautiously around them because, one can speculate, parents who could do that are capable of almost anything (O'Hanlon and Hudson, 1994). Humorous Ericksonian interventions were playful, and at the same time harmless (not mean-spirited). It is important to use humour that is supportive and affirming, not humour that is demeaning in any way.

Drama

Erickson's use of drama was liberal – he did dramatic things and he had his patients do dramatic things. In Chapter 2, we discussed the case of the man who learned to drive by fainting at the wheel, which is an excellent example of a dramatic ordeal directive, which provided a new experiential base from which the patient could respond to old problems. Dramatic applications could be direct or indirect, as well as active or passive. As Carol Lankton wrote about Erickson:

> He illustrated (often at great length) the experiences he wanted his clients to retrieve as they fixated their attention upon the dramatic aspects of an unfolding story line about someone else. Clients were free to create their own meaning from the stimulus offered and even have learnings too painful for the conscious mind to tolerate. After all, it was 'only a story.' (1985: 68)

At the conclusion of *Uncommon Therapy*, Jay Haley recounted a poignant case with a dramatic intervention and dramatic results. A woman had travelled to see Erickson from California with her husband who had been completely paralysed by a stroke a year earlier. He was a Prussian German, very proud with a long history of competence and achievement. Subsequent to his stroke he was told repeatedly that he could never recover. By the time his wife brought him to see Erickson, he had not been able to speak for an entire year. After learning about the man's history from the wife, Erickson told the woman that he would help, but that she must agree not to interfere. She consented and the man was carried into Erickson's office. Erickson berated and insulted the man at length, calling him names such as 'a dirty Nazi', 'lazy', 'a charity case', 'stupid', 'conceited' and 'ignorant'. Throughout this process the man's rage was obviously building. Finally, Erickson said he hadn't been fully prepared, and that the man would have to come back the next day so that he could be properly berated. At that point, the patient exploded, 'No' . . . his first spoken word in a year. Erickson continued his tirade, and the patient repeating, 'No, no, no!', somehow forced himself out of his seat, staggered to the door and even down the steps, and managed to crawl into the car in which he had come. He returned the next day, and he and Erickson began, this time in a friendly and collaborative way, the process of his recovery. Over the course of two months, he made partial recoveries in his ability to walk, speak, use his arm and read. He returned to the business he had built, under the agreement that he would only undertake simpler and less taxing duties (Haley, 1973).

The Impact of Humour and Drama
Erickson often used humour and drama as part of his therapeutic arsenal. Similarly, a review of current approaches in the field shows

that dramatic interventions have become part of the psychother-apeutic culture. Behavioural approaches may have individuals con-front their feared stimuli; cognitive/behavioural approaches may have an individual carry out task assignments in order to create a new sense of competence (sometimes in a humorous and self-effacing way); Gestalt approaches may have a patient role play and speak to the empty chair; and Psychodrama creatively enacts conflict-laden scenes in ways that alter the participant's perspectives and options.

It would be inaccurate to suggest that Erickson is solely respon-sible for the development of drama and humour in therapy; he was merely in a position to be an innovator at a time when those approaches were not commonly used. The use of humour and drama would have emerged in other quarters of the psychotherapeutic arena without Erickson's contribution. What *is* unique is the integration of humour and drama within Erickson's communication style. Thus, for example, we see that a dramatic Ericksonian inter-vention may be delivered entirely as a metaphor, or an ordeal may be experienced through hypnotic hallucination and subsequent amnesia. Whatever the case, the hallmark of the Ericksonian dra-matic or humorous intervention was that it drew upon, and appealed to, the individual's unique strengths and resources. The social context of the patient also was emphasized in Erickson's work.

Social Context

Increased attention to the social/physical context within which human functioning occurs is another of Erickson's major contribu-tions to the field of psychotherapy. Erickson included the patient's life circumstances in the assessment and treatment process. In formulating his interventions, he considered the physical and social environment that either maintained the problem, and/or could be utilized to resolve the problem. Erickson even provided treatment in the patient's home when necessary. This break with the orthodox treatment of his day has been validated by the fact that home-based treatment is used in contemporary practice and is no longer contraindicated.

When Erickson began practising, the three existent major schools of therapy paid little or no attention to the social domain within which a patient functioned; psychoanalysis concerned itself with past conflicts; behaviourists were interested in the social context only to the degree that it was an antecedent stimulus; and the 'third force', humanistic therapy, provided a therapeutic environment in the office so that the patient's natural healing processes might unfold. None of the three involved family members in the therapy process. None of them suggested interventions that would occur at home or in the work setting, and house calls were unheard of. In formulating his interventions, Erickson did not limit therapy to the office.

One could suggest that Erickson was attuned to the concept of 'continuum of care', which is jargon commonly used today by behavioural health-care payers, who view remedying the problem in the home as a superior (and cheaper) alternative to in-patient care. Erickson made house calls throughout his career, or at least until his health no longer permitted it. Perhaps he simply recognized that it was more humane to see bed-ridden cancer patients in their home for pain control, as opposed to requiring patients to be brought to him.

As asserted earlier, Erickson did marriage and family therapy when his peers would not because of theoretical constraints that could only accommodate a therapeutic unit of one. In a conversation with John Weakland and Jay Haley about including a family who might be prone to reject an invitation to join the therapy, Erickson said:

> You always have to try for what you think is the most comprehensive and the best, recognizing that maybe you're not going to get any cooperation. You always try to find out from your patient just how the other person at home reacts. The other person will try to probe and find out what happens in therapy. Sometimes you feed the other person's curiosity. You say to a woman, here and there, that you don't know just how her husband would feel about such and such. It is something she can mention to her husband. Her husband has got to formulate what he is told. He's got to decide how to think about it. The next time she'll tell you how he responded, and you can reconstrue his utterance. The first thing he knows, he's beginning to recognize that he has got to come in and straighten you out on a number of things. So he insists that his wife make an appointment for him. (Haley, 1985b: 147)

Erickson would often gear his interventions to the patient's customary environment, even when the sessions were all conducted in his office. For example, he might orient a patient to a positive vocational future through hypnotic hallucination of that outcome in the current workplace. Earlier in this chapter, we described the female psychiatrist who had poor grooming skills. One intervention established a new dimension to her customary environment (the makeup counter at the local department store) and another utilized her work environment (the staff dance).

Erickson also was aware of when to eliminate aspects of the social context. In one case, he was consulted by a physician for assistance with her 18-year-old son's acne. He instructed her to take him on their customary Christmas ski holiday, and to ensure that he was exposed to no mirrors in the cabin or elsewhere during the two week period. The acne cleared up (O'Hanlon and Hexum, 1990). Erickson's intervention was that of 'an old-time doc'. It would not occur to many therapists, and certainly would not be generated through application of the principles of the major psychotherapeutic theories.

Today, home-based family therapy is becoming increasingly common. Wrap-around treatment programmes enlist the patient's family, school, church and recreational milieu in the therapy process. Contemporary practitioners utilize the support, strengths and commitment from relevant family/community members to optimize the patient's success. One cannot solely credit Erickson for developing a home-based treatment approach, yet he was among the first to use it. Remember the African Violet Queen of Milwaukee – there was a house call to a patient's aunt, and an intervention that involved a broad spectrum of the community, including interaction by the patient at transition points in the individual community members' lives including marriages, engagements, births and deaths.

Home/community-based, family-oriented treatment was a direct result of Erickson's attention to his patient's day-to-day environment. Erickson was committed to utilizing any aspects of the patient's environment that could be incorporated into the treatment process. He affirmed the usefulness of working with the patient's social context, and his unique and custom-tailored interventions were a hallmark of Erickson's work that led to his worldwide following.

Worldwide Following

A rapid momentum and acceleration developed around the acceptance of Erickson's work, especially in the 1970s and thereafter. This rapid growth reflected the readiness on the part of the psychotherapeutic community to step beyond theoretical constraints and to see patients as unique, and capable of participating actively in their own treatment through the use of experiential methods of change.

Erickson was renowned in hypnosis circles in his early career. By the 1940s, Erickson had gained a reputation as a dedicated hypnosis researcher, and an authority on hypnosis and hypnotic therapy. During the 1950s and early 1960s, he taught and lectured internationally to professional groups. In 1973, *Uncommon Therapy:*

The Psychiatric Techniques of Milton H. Erickson, MD was published by Jay Haley, and awareness of his work expanded expo-
nentially. Further publications by Erickson, Rossi and Haley fuelled
the process. During the late 1970s, professionals made their way to
Phoenix to learn from the 'Sage in the Desert'.

By 1978, plans were underway for the First International Congress on Ericksonian Approaches to Hypnosis and Psychotherapy.
More than 2000 people attended that meeting, in spite of the fact
that Erickson died nearly nine months before it took place. It was
scheduled to have been a celebration of Erickson's 78th birthday,
and an opportunity for him to once more see his friends, but instead
it became the inception of the Milton H. Erickson Foundation.
Erickson, himself, was one of the founding board members, along
with his wife, Elizabeth, and Jeffrey Zeig and his then wife, Sherron
Peters.

The Foundation, located in Phoenix, is dedicated to promoting
and advancing Ericksonian approaches to hypnosis and psychotherapy. It also makes a substantial contribution to the advancement of
the field of psychotherapy in general. The Foundation's Mission
Statement reads as follows:

> The mission of The Milton H. Erickson Foundation, Inc. is to provide
> educational programs designed for professionals in the health sciences. It
> is to further the worldwide understanding and practice of medical and
> clinical hypnosis and hypnotherapy by promoting in every ethical way
> the contributions made in the field by the late Milton H. Erickson, M.D.
> It is to integrate Ericksonian techniques into all reputable fields of
> psychotherapy and through this, it is to promote the further evolution of
> psychotherapy and health sciences. The Erickson Foundation is
> committed to developing, preserving and maintaining the Erickson
> Archives which relate to the previously stated mission.

The Foundation has an archive of information (books, audio
recordings and video recordings of, and about, Erickson and other
master therapists), which can be accessed by scholars. The Foundation sponsors meetings – at least one major conference annually –
on topics such as the Evolution of Psychotherapy, Brief Therapy,
Ericksonian Therapy, as well as regional conferences on Couples
Therapy and Sex Therapy. Five-day intensive seminars on Ericksonian Hypnotherapy at the beginning, intermediate and advanced
levels are conducted three times a year. The Foundation also pub-
lishes a Newsletter and has published 10 books of proceedings from
its various conferences. There is a web site on the Internet: http://
www.erickson-foundation.org.

If one can use the existence of an Ericksonian Institute in a
geographical region as an indicator of interest, then interest is high

both in the United States and abroad. As of 1998, there are more than 75 affiliated institutes around the world. These institutes are dedicated to providing training, supervision and treatment. They are a forum for the exchange of information and ideas.

Conferences
The Foundation has dedicated its large conferences to one of three agendas: Ericksonian Methods of Hypnosis and Psychotherapy, Brief Therapy Approaches and The Evolution of Psychotherapy. These conferences, attended by therapists from around the world, have contributed significantly to both practitioner skill development and growth within the field. At these meetings, innovators teach about their work and train practitioners in the practical application of their approach.

The Evolution of Psychotherapy conferences are held in the United States every five years (1985, 1990, 1995, . . .). The conference was held once in Europe (1994). It has featured the leaders in contemporary therapy, including such luminaries as Aaron T. Beck, Bruno Bettelheim, Murray Bowen, James F.T. Bugental, Albert Ellis, Victor Frankl, Eugene Gendlin, William Glasser, Mary M. and Robert Goulding, Jay Haley, James Hillman, Otto F. Kernberg, R.D. Laing, Arnold A. Lazarus, Alexander Lowen, Cloé Madanes, Judd Marmor, James F. Masterson, Rollo May, Donald Meichenbaum, Salvador Minuchin, Zerka Moreno, Mara Selvini Palazzoli, Erving and Miriam Polster, Carl R. Rogers, Ernest L. Rossi, Virginia M. Satir, Thomas S. Szasz, Paul Watzlawick, Carl A. Whitaker, Lewis R. Wolberg, Joseph Wolpe, Irving Yalom and Jeffrey K. Zeig.

The Brief Therapy conferences, held approximately every three years, bring together experts from disparate approaches, including brief psychodynamic therapy, gestalt therapy, cognitive therapy, Ericksonian therapy, etc. First held in 1988, it is the premier multidisciplinary meeting on short-term approaches.

Panels at conferences have brought together divergent views of difficult problems. For example, at one of the conferences, when Christine Padesky (a cognitive behaviourist) discussed her work with borderline personality disorders on a panel with James Masterson (founder of the Masterson Institute, and author of several definitive texts on the psychodynamic approach to the treatment of personality disorders), he challenged her with a case example of an individual who chronically found herself to be excluded and victimized. How, Masterson wondered, did Padesky respond to the patient's (mis-)interpretation of peers' simple conversation as indicative of dislike for her. Padesky responded that she would acknowledge the possibility that the people in the patient's world disliked her, then go on to ask what *else* the peers' comments might mean. Masterson paused, considering this response, then said that he liked it and might use it. In this panel, Psychodynamic and Cognitive/behavioural proponents engaged in dialogue with a shared vision resulting. This is only one instance of how these conferences promote rapprochement within the field of psychotherapy, and are in line with Erickson's personal philosophy and atheoretical view. Once theoretical 'secular' barriers are dispensed with, what remains are multiple views of various aspects of the whole patient. In this way, the Foundation's conferences, which foster theoretical integration, are truly 'Ericksonian'.

In addition to the 'integrative conferences', six congresses on Ericksonian Approaches to Hypnosis and Psychotherapy have been held since 1980, and the seventh is scheduled for 1999. In intervening years, smaller Erickson Seminars are held. These congresses attract 1000–2000 people and the seminars, up to 700. They bring together leading practitioners and have helped advance the scope and practice of Ericksonian methods.

In addition to its training opportunities, the Foundation sponsors a Newsletter, web page, a listserv, all of which provide a wealth of information about Erickson and his work to interested practitioners. The sheer scope and volume of these resources attest to the interest in Erickson on a worldwide scale, which has also spawned derivative schools.

Derivative Schools

There is no question that Erickson was a profound influence in a great many quarters, and where that influence is clearly seminal, we have labelled the approach as a derivative school of thought. Through his association with Gregory Bateson, the Mental Research Institute (MRI) sought out Erickson's ideas on communication. Haley and Madanes developed their Strategic approach, based on Erickson's ideas. Neuro-Linguistic Programming is, in part, derived from an analysis of Erickson's communication patterns and style. Rossi's Mind–Body work is predicated on what he learned about physiological changes that occurred in patients during hypnosis.

Erickson's success and creativity spawned a variety of approaches. A significant number of his students (and their students) have developed and articulated aspects of their approach that in many ways builds on their training with Erickson. These Ericksonians include Jeff Zeig, Stephen and Carol Lankton, Stephen Gilligan and William O'Hanlon, as well as Neo-Ericksonians whose work is grounded in Ericksonian principles, but who never studied with him directly, such as Michael Yapko.

Mental Research Institute

From 1952 to 1962, Gregory Bateson headed up a research project on communication. The research team consisted of Jay Haley and John Weakland (research assistants) and Don D. Jackson and William F. Fry (consulting psychiatrists). The parameters of that project were broad: the team could investigate anything as long as it illuminated some aspect of the paradoxes that arise in the communication process. Erickson's influence on that project began in the mid-1950s. Bateson wrote Erickson a five-page letter outlining the double bind and asking Erickson about similarities between the actions of the hypnotist and the binds of schizophrenic families. Bateson introduced Jay Haley and John Weakland to Erickson, and subsequently Haley attended one of Erickson's seminars on hypnosis. At the time, the project was examining, among other things, how it is that specific communication patterns maintain pathology. Theirs was a homeostatic model, which described family structure and communication patterns quite well, but which was more anthropological and descriptive than an investigation of the change process in therapy.

Jay Haley and John Weakland, through their early contacts with Erickson, became enamoured with the idea of brief treatment approaches, and Haley eventually developed the strategic school, while Weakland who remained at MRI was one of the founders of their 'interactional approach'. At the time of those first meetings with Erickson, therapy was dominated by psychoanalytic thinking. In contrast, Erickson who was decidedly directive, achieved results quickly. Haley and Weakland learned about ordeals, family-based interventions, hypnosis, tasks and metaphors. The directive nature of strategic interventions transforms the therapist role from passive to active, and radically increases the probability of the treatment succeeding in a short period of time. Haley and Weakland carried back what they learned from Erickson to Palo Alto, and the foundation was established for what would, in 1967, become the Brief Therapy Center at MRI. Here Erickson's work continued to impact the thinking of individuals such as Paul Watzlawick, Don Jackson and Richard Fisch.

Strategic/Solution-focused Treatment

Haley broke off from the Palo Alto group and went to the Philadelphia Child Guidance Clinic where he collaborated with the founder of structural family therapy, Salvador Minuchin, and with

Braulio Montalvo. Haley developed strategic family systems interventions, which especially attended to the hierarchies and the distribution of influence within the family structure. Ultimately, he established the Family Therapy Institute of Washington, DC, and was joined by Cloé Madanes.

In 1969, Steve de Shazer began his investigation into brief treatment. In *Keys to Solutions in Brief Therapy* (1985), de Shazer cites some of Erickson's work as seminal in his approach to brief treatment:

> As I see it, this is the key to brief therapy: *Utilizing what the client brings with him to meet his needs in such a way that the client can make a satisfactory life for himself.* As Erickson put it, no attempt was made to correct any 'causative under-lying maladjustments,' and none was needed. (1985: 6)

Erickson's focus on strategic problem-solving is evident in much of de Shazer's early work. He also incorporated Erickson's notion of creating a positive vision of the future into his work; this is embodied in his 'miracle question' – 'If you woke up tomorrow, and your problem was miraculously solved, how would things be different?' De Shazer has become a major force in the brief treatment movement.

Neuro-linguistic Programming

Richard Bandler, a therapist, with John Grinder, a linguist, developed a communications-based approach to hypnosis and treatment, called Neuro-Linguistic Programming. They used the transformational grammar of Noam Chomsky and other tools to methodically examine the communication patterns present in Erickson and other experts. Milton Erickson's work and case studies were a major focus of their analysis. They published *Patterns of the Hypnotic Techniques of Milton H. Erickson MD, Vol. I*, in 1975. Erickson's influence is present in much of their writings, and has influenced the chief expositors of NLP, including Robert Dilts, who has been a prolific author and teacher.

Rossi's Mind–Body Work

Ernest Rossi, who started as a Jungian analyst, worked with Milton Erickson first as a patient, then as a student, and finally as a collaborator. Rossi was Erickson's Boswell. He edited a major portion of Erickson's writings into collections that included Erickson's commentary, and wrote about Erickson as well. Subsequently, Rossi developed his own approach that explored psychoneuroimmunology. He vigorously explored the connection between mind and body, and developed a model that accesses unconscious resources to aid in the healing process. Further, he encourages patients to utilize natural body rhythms to augment healing and growth.

Neo-Ericksonians
Many individuals influenced by Erickson continue to contribute to the field in a substantial way. The single disclaimer here is this – as was always the case with Erickson's therapy, the evolution of his approach, even today, is a work in progress. Haley, Weakland, Fisch, Jackson, Watzlawick, Bandler and Grinder, Rossi and de Shazer have been previously identified as having developed derivative schools. The distinction between this group (derivative schools) and the remainder of the 'Neo-Ericksonian' group is somewhat arbitrary. It is likely that over time, the work of many of the individuals discussed in the ensuing section may well evolve into distinct derivative schools.

Jeffrey Zeig has articulated a metamodel for understanding the communications process that is implicit in Ericksonian hypnosis and therapy (Zeig, 1992). He has elucidated the 'seeding' process by which Erickson began implementing the intervention well in advance of any induction or assignment (Zeig, 1990a). He has written prolifically on utilization (Zeig, 1992), on his experiences with Erickson (Zeig, 1985; Zeig and Geary, 1990), and on various aspects of psychotherapy in general (Zeig and Munion, 1990). In addition to this writing, he is President of the Board of Directors of The Milton H. Erickson Foundation. In this capacity, he is involved in planning all the conferences and training sponsored by the Erickson Foundation.

Stephen and Carol Lankton were students of Erickson. Stephen was the founding editor of The Milton H. Erickson Foundation's *Ericksonian Monograph* series, which examined therapy related topics from the perspective of various Ericksonian therapists, and reviewed relevant publications. The Lanktons have written about hypnosis (1983) and Ericksonian techniques in family therapy (Lankton and Lankton, 1986). Both are quite active in providing training in Ericksonian methods.

William O'Hanlon published significant books about Erickson's work (O'Hanlon, 1987; O'Hanlon and Hexum, 1990), and Ericksonian methods of therapy. In particular, O'Hanlon has worked with developing solution-focused treatment approaches (Cade and O'Hanlon, 1993; O'Hanlon and Weiner-Davis, 1989; O'Hanlon and Martin, 1992). He continues to be very active in writing, training and practice. Joseph Barber (Barber, 1977a, 1977b, 1980, 1987, 1989, 1993; Barber and Adrian, 1982; Price and Barber,

1987) has contributed substantially in terms of pain management techniques and hypnosis, and has been a perennial faculty member at the Ericksonian Congresses. Michael Yapko (1988, 1989, 1992) has distinguished himself with his writing on the subjects of hypnosis, brief therapy and depression. He also has written articulately on directive therapy (Yapko, 1990).

The late Kay F. Thompson, also a student of Erickson, was a leader and teacher in the application of hypnosis for pain control in dentistry. Stephen Gilligan has trained students in Ericksonian methods for 20 years, and has written about these methods (Gilligan, 1993; Gilligan and Price, 1987; Zeig and Gilligan, 1990; Lankton *et al.*, 1991). His current work has evolved to his 'Self-Relations' approach to therapy which has the promise of becoming its own free standing school (Gilligan, 1997). Ericksonian principles as applied to the treatment of chronic and resistant patients, as well as sexual abuse survivors, have been advanced cogently by Yvonne Dolan (1985, 1986, 1989, 1991, 1997). John and Janet Edgette (1995) have written thoughtfully about hypnosis. Daniel Araoz (1985), and others including Herb Lustig, Sidney Rosen, Betty Alice Erickson, Phillip and Norma Baretta . . . the list is seemingly endless . . . have all been influenced by Erickson, and have gone on to train others in this effective method of treatment.

Conclusion

While it is widely acknowledged that Erickson was a master hypnotist (Zilbergeld *et al.*, 1986; Weitzenhoffer, 1989), perhaps the impact of Erickson's hypnosis is better understood in the broader context of his therapy. D. Corydon Hammond (1986) assessed the validity of the claims that Erickson was a superlatively effective therapist, and did an admirable job of the task. He presented a balanced account that declined to deify Erickson or to hold him to a standard other than those used to assess the quality of any therapist's work. Hammond pointed out that, as with most therapists, we have no empirical data about Erickson's 'effectiveness rate'. He concluded:

> Although we will never know exactly how successful Erickson was as a therapist, just as we don't know how successful any other therapists are, I think the weight of the evidence is that Erickson was one of the best. He had qualities that any good therapist would do well to emulate! He worked to convey understanding, was respectful and willing to accept patients where they were. He was not a 'hypnotist' who believed in hypnosis or any other method as a panacea. Hypnosis was just one part

of his work. He was an exceptional model of eclecticism, willing to use almost anything that might be helpful. He always attempted to individualize treatment to suit the patient rather than attempting to fit the patient into the mold of the therapist's theory or favorite method. He was concerned with what worked and not with what fit or didn't fit into this or that model of therapy. He was also uniquely dedicated to the patients he worked with and cared enough to devote enormous amounts of time to thoughtful treatment planning and introspective analysis of his own behavior. He was persistent, and resistance was not perceived as a problem of the patient, but as a challenge to his creativity and flexibility. I consider these to be qualities of excellence. (1986: 235)

So do the authors of this text.

The future of Ericksonian-inspired approaches is bright. Students continue to seek training, new aspects of Erickson's wisdom continue to be elucidated and new derivative methods are advanced. The legacy of Milton Erickson continues to shape the direction of contemporary practice.

Bibliography of Erickson-inspired Books and Books from the Milton H. Erickson Foundation

Alman, B. and Lambrou, P. (1991) *Self-hypnosis: The Complete Manual for Health and Self-change* (2nd edn). New York: Brunner/Mazel.

Bandler, R. and Grinder, J. (1975) *Patterns of the Hypnotic Techniques of Milton H. Erickson, MD* (Vol. 1). Cupertino, CA: Meta Publications.

This is a how-to manual for reproducing Erickson's use of language in trance inductions. The model presented is based on transformational grammar and split-brain research.

Bauer, Sofia M.F. (1998) *Hipnoterapia Ericksoniana paso a paso*. Campinas/SP Brazil: Editora Psy (in Portuguese).

Bell-Gadsby, Cheryl and Siegenberg, Anne (1996) *Reclaiming her Story: Ericksonian Solution-focused Therapy for Sexual Abuse*. New York: Brunner/Mazel.

Combs, G. and Freedman, J. (1990) *Symbol, Story and Ceremony: Using Metaphor in Individual and Family Therapy*. New York: Norton.

The authors illustrate the artistic and metaphorical side of Ericksonian psychotherapy.

Cooper, L. and Erickson, M. (1982) *Time Distortion in Hypnosis* (2nd edn). New York: Irvington.

The results of Erickson's and Cooper's experimental and clinical work in this area. Much of this material is included in the *Collected Papers*.

Dolan, Y. (1985) *A Path with a Heart: Ericksonian Utilization with Resistant and Chronic Clients*. New York: Brunner/Mazel.

This book presents an extension of Ericksonian principles and techniques into work with difficult, multi-problem, long-term patients.

Dolan, Y. (1991) *Resolving Sexual Abuse: Solution-focused Therapy and Ericksonian Hypnosis for Adult Survivors*. New York: Norton.

Edgette, J. and Edgette, J. (1995) *The Handbook of Hypnotic Phenomena in Psychotherapy*. New York: Brunner/Mazel.

Erickson, M., Hershman, S. and Secter, I. (1989) *The Practical Application of Medical and Dental Hypnosis* (3rd edn). New York: Brunner/Mazel.

This book was compiled primarily from transcripts of workshops for medical, psychological and dental professionals given by the authors during the late 1950s. It was reissued in 1989 with a foreword by Jeffrey K. Zeig, PhD.

Erickson, M., Rossi, E. and Rossi, S. (1976) *Hypnotic Realities: The Induction of Clinical Hypnosis and Forms of Indirect Suggestions*. New York: Irvington.

The first book in a series of three co-authored by Erickson and Rossi. Gives an overall model for Erickson's hypnotic approaches. Contains numerous discussions and commentaries on transcripts of inductions. Accompanied by an audiocassette of Erickson doing two inductions with the same subject.

Erickson, M. and Rossi, E. (1979) *Hyponotherapy: An Exploratory Casebook*. New York: Irvington.

The second book in the series. This volume deals extensively with hypnotic therapy, utilizing numerous case examples and transcripts. A tape of a therapy session, conducted by Erickson, with a man with phantom limb pain and his wife with tinnitus accompanies this book.

Erickson, M. and Rossi, E. (1981) *Experiencing Hypnosis: Therapeutic Approaches to Altered State*. New York: Irvington.

The third book in the series, containing a transcript of a lecture on hypnosis in psychiatry by Erickson and discussion of various therapeutic techniques and approaches. Includes a description of Erickson's famous non-verbal arm catalepsy induction technique. Two audiocassettes (of the lecture mentioned above) accompany this book.

Erickson, M. and Rossi, E. (1989) *The February Man: Evolving Consciousness and Identity in Hypnotherapy*. New York: Brunner/Mazel.
Gilligan, S.G. (1986) *Therapeutic Trances: The Cooperation Principle in Ericksonian Hypnotherapy*. New York: Brunner/Mazel.

This book is Gilligan's overview of Ericksonian hypnotherapy, including his model of symptom phenomena as self-devaluing trance phenomena and how to transform them into self-valuing assets. A general discussion of the major schools of hypnosis is included to put Erickson's approach into context.

Gordon, D. (1978) *Therapeutic Metaphors: Helping Others Through the Looking Glass*. Cupertino, CA: Meta Publications.
Gordon, D. and Myers-Anderson, M. (1981) *Phoenix: Therapeutic Patterns of Milton H. Erickson*. Cupertino, CA: Meta Publications.

An attempt at systematizing and making explicit Erickson's therapeutic (as opposed to strictly hypnotic) work. Uses material from Erickson's teaching seminars to illustrate the principles discussed.

Grinder, J., DeLozier, J. and Bandler, R. (1977) *Patterns of the Hypnotic Techniques of Milton H. Erickson, M.D.*, Vol. II. Cupertino, CA: Meta Publications.

This second book in the series offers conceptions of sensory-based maps, different approaches for congruent and incongruent clients and other ideas about Erickson's hypnotic work. A transcript of Erickson's work (taken from 'The Artistry of Milton Erickson' videotape) is analysed with reference to the formulations presented in both volumes.

Haley, J. (1963) *Strategies of Psychotherapy*. New York: Grune & Stratton.
Haley, J. (ed.) (1967) *Advanced Techniques of Hypnosis and Therapy: Selected Papers of Milton H. Erickson, MD*. New York: Grune & Stratton.

This was the first effort to compile Erickson's major papers on hypnosis and therapy. It also contains a biographical introduction and discussion of Erickson's work by Haley, Erickson's longtime student and popularizer. All of this material, with the exception of Haley's writing, is included in the *Collected Papers* (edited by Rossi).

Haley, J. (1973) *Uncommon Therapy: The Psychiatric Techniques of Milton H. Erickson, MD*. New York: Norton.

Contains numerous case examples, discussions with Erickson, commentaries and specific techniques. The book is mainly about Erickson's therapeutic approaches. The material is organized and presented within the family life cycle framework.

Haley, J. (1976) *Problem Solving Therapy*. San Franscisco: Jossey-Bass.
Haley, J. (1984) *Ordeal Therapy*. San Francisco: Jossey-Bass.

This is an extension of the benevolent ordeal therapy Haley learned from Erickson. Some Erickson cases are used, but the majority comes from cases Haley supervised or treated himself.

Haley, J. (1985a) *Conversations with Milton H. Erickson, MD, Vol. I: Changing Individuals*. New York: Triangle (Norton).
Haley, J. (1985b) *Conversations with Milton H. Erickson, MD, Vol. II: Changing Couples*. New York: Triangle (Norton).
Haley, J. (1985c) *Conversations with Milton H. Erickson, MD, Vol. III: Changing Children and Families*. New York: Triangle (Norton).

These conversations took place mainly in the late 1950s between Erickson, Haley, John Weakland and occasionally Gregory Bateson. Haley and Weakland were trying to understand Erickson's brief therapy for their research with Bateson's project on communication and for their own clinical work with individuals, couples and families. Reading the books is like reading the transcripts of supervision sessions with some theoretical material and some case discussion. This material was the source for much of the material in *Uncommon Therapy*.

Haley, J. (1993) *Jay Haley on Milton H. Erickson*. New York: Brunner/Mazel.
Havens, R. (1985) *The Wisdom of Milton H. Erickson*. New York: Irvington.

This book is a compilation of quotations from Erickson on various topics relating to therapy and hypnosis. The quotations are organized into sections, and what emerges constitutes a natural model for Erickson's therapeutic and hypnotic approaches.

Havens, Ronald A. (ed.) (1992) *The Wisdom of Milton Erickson: Human Behavior and Psychotherapy*, Vol. II. New York: Irvington Publishers.
Havens, R. and Walters, C. (1989) *Hypnotherapy Scripts: A Neo-Ericksonian Approach to Persuasive Healing*. New York: Brunner/Mazel.
Kershaw, C. (1992) *The Couple's Hypnotic Dance: Creating Ericksonian Strategies in Marital Therapy*. New York: Brunner/Mazel.
Klippstein, H. (ed.) (1991) *Ericksonian Hypnotherapeutic Group Inductions*. New York: Brunner/Mazel.
Lankton, C. and Lankton, S. (1989) *Tales of Enchantment: Goal-oriented Metaphors for Adults and Children in Therapy*. New York: Brunner/Mazel.
Lankton, S. (1980) *Practical Magic: A Translation of Basic Neurolinguistic Programming into Clinical Psychotherapy*. Cupertino, CA: Meta Publications.

Lankton, S. (ed.) (1985) *Ericksonian Monographs Number I: Elements and Dimensions of an Ericksonian Approach.* New York: Brunner/Mazel.

This is the first volume in a continuing series of *Ericksonian Monographs*, sponsored by The Milton H. Erickson Foundation as a forum for continuing education and information exchange. This volume contains a variety of articles on different applications of Erickson's work. It includes a new article, contributed by Elizabeth Erickson, that is an update of an unpublished Milton Erickson article on certain principles of medical hypnosis.

Lankton, S. (ed.) (1987) *Ericksonian Monographs Number 2: Central Themes and Principles of Ericksonian Therapy.* New York: Brunner/Mazel.

This is the second of the *Ericksonian Monographs series*, including nine articles and three book reviews.

Lankton, S. (ed.) (1989) *Ericksonian Monographs Number 5: Ericksonian Hypnosis: Application, Preparation and Research.* New York: Brunner/Mazel.

Lankton, S. and Erickson, K. (eds) (1993) *Ericksonian Monographs Number 9: The Essence of a Single Session Success.* New York: Brunner/Mazel.

Lankton, S., Gilligan, S. and Zeig, J. (eds) (1991) *Ericksonian Monographs Number 8: Views on Ericksonian Brief Therapy, Process and Action.* New York: Brunner/Mazel.

Lankton, S. and Lankton, C. (1983) *The Answer Within: A Clinical Framework of Ericksonian Hypnotherapy.* New York: Brunner/Mazel.

Contains case examples from Erickson's and the Lanktons' work embedded in a comprehensive framework to provide clinicians access to Ericksonian approaches to the use of hypnosis in therapy.

Lankton, S. and Lankton, C. (1986) *Enchantment and Intervention in Family Therapy: Training in Ericksonian Approaches.* New York: Brunner/Mazel.

This book takes the Lanktons' elaboration of Erickson's work further than the first book and links the hypnotic approaches to family and couple therapy.

Lankton, S., Lankton, C. and Matthews, W. (1991) 'Ericksonian family therapy', in A. Gurman and D. Kniskern (eds), *The Handbook of Family Therapy*, Vol. II. New York: Brunner/Mazel.

Lankton, S. and Zeig, J. (eds) (1988) *Ericksonian Monographs Number 3: Treatment of Special Populations with Ericksonian Approaches.* New York: Brunner/Mazel.

Lankton, S. and Zeig, J. (eds) (1988) *Ericksonian Monographs Number 4: Research, Comparisons and Medical Applications of Ericksonian Techniques.* New York: Brunner/Mazel.

Lankton, S. and Zeig, J. (eds) (1989) *Ericksonian Monographs Number 6: Extrapolations: Demonstrations of Ericksonian Therapy.* New York: Brunner/Mazel.

Lankton, S. and Zeig, J. (eds) (1995) *Ericksonian Monographs Number 10: Difficult Contexts for Therapy.* New York: Brunner/Mazel.

Leva, R. (ed.) (1988) *Psychotherapy: The Listening Voice: Rogers and Erickson.* Muncie, IN: Accelerated Development.

Loriedo, C. and Vella, G. (1992) *Paradox and the Family System.* New York: Brunner/Mazel.

Lovern, J.D. (1991) *Pathways to Reality: Erickson-inspired Treatment Approaches to Chemical Dependency*. New York: Brunner/Mazel.

Lustig, H. (1975) *The Artistry of Milton H. Erickson, MD (Part 1 and Part 2)*. Haverford, PA: Herbert S. Lustig, MD, Ltd., a videotape of Erickson conducting hypnosis.

Matthews, W.J. and Edgette, John H. (eds) (1997) *Current Thinking and Research in Brief Therapy: Solutions, Strategies, Narratives*, Vol. I. New York: Brunner/Mazel.

Matthews, W.J. and Edgette, John H. (eds) (1998) *Current Thinking and Research in Brief Therapy: Solutions, Strategies, Narratives*, Vol. II. New York: Brunner/Mazel.

Mehl, L. and Peterson, G. (1989) *The Art of Healing*. New York: Irvington.

Mills, J., Crowley, R. and Ryan, M. (1986) *Therapeutic Metaphors for Children and the Child Within*. New York: Brunner/Mazel.

O'Hanlon, W.H. (1987) *Taproots: Underlying Principles of Milton Erickson's Therapy and Hypnosis*. New York: Norton.

O'Hanlon, W.H. and Hexum, A.L. (1990) *An Uncommon Casebook: The Complete Clinical Work of Milton H. Erickson*. New York: Norton.

O'Hanlon, W.H. and Martin, M. (1992) *Solution-oriented Hypnosis: An Ericksonian Approach*. New York: Norton.

Overholser, L. (1984) *Ericksonian Hypnosis: Handbook of Clinical Practice*. New York: Irvington.

This is a primer on the induction and therapeutic use of hypnosis using an Ericksonian approach. It includes exercises at the end of each chapter to practise the skills discussed.

Phillips, M. and Frederick, C. (1995) *Healing the Divided Self: Clinical and Ericksonian Hypnotherapy for Post Traumatic and Dissociative Conditions*. New York: Norton.

Ritterman, M. (1983) *Using Hypnosis in Family Therapy*. San Francisco: Jossey-Bass.

Robles, T. (1990) *A Concert for Four Hemispheres in Psychotherapy*. Mexico City: Institute of Milton H. Erickson de la Ciudad de Mexico. New York: Vantage Press.

Robles, T. (1991) *Terapia cortada a la medida: un seminario ericksoniano con Jeffrey K. Zeig*. Mexico City: Institute of Milton H. Erickson de la Ciudad de Mexico (in Spanish).

Rosen, S. (ed.) (1982) *My Voice Will Go with You: The Teaching Tales of Milton H. Erickson*. New York: Norton.

Rossi, E. (ed.) (1980) *The Collected Papers of Milton H. Erickson on Hypnosis. Vol. I: The Nature of Hypnosis and Suggestion; Vol. II: Hypnotic Alteration of Sensory, Perceptual and Psychophysiological Processes; Vol. III: Hypnotic Investigation of Psychodynamic Processes; Vol. IV: Innovative Hypnotherapy*. New York: Irvington.

This four-volume work includes all of Erickson's published papers on hypnosis and therapy, some previously unpublished material, and a few papers by Erickson's collaborators (Ernest Rossi, Elizabeth Erickson, Jeffrey Zeig and others).

Rossi, E., Ryan, M. and Sharp, F. (eds) (1983) *Healing in Hypnosis: The Seminars, Workshops and Lectures of Milton H. Erickson*, Vol. I. New York: Irvington.

This is the first in a four-volume series of transcripts of Erickson's lectures and demonstrations from the 1950s and 1960s. This volume also contains a short biography and some pictures of Erickson over the years. It is accompanied by a tape of one of the lectures transcribed in the book.

Rossi, E. and Ryan, M. (eds) (1985) *Life Reframing in Hypnosis: The Seminars, Workshops and Lectures of Milton H. Erickson*, Vol. II. New York: Irvington.

This is a continuation of the volume above. A tape of Erickson doing hypnotic therapy with a photographer is included.

Rossi, E. and Ryan, M. (eds) (1986) *Mind–Body Communication in Hypnosis: The Seminars, Workshops and Lectures of Milton H. Erickson* (Vol. III). New York: Irvington.

The third volume of this edited series is mainly focused on Erickson's work with somatic problems and issues.

Rossi, E. and Ryan, M. (1991) *Creative Choice in Hypnosis: The Seminars, Workshops and Lectures of Milton H. Erickson*, Vol. IV. New York: Irvington.

A collection of some of Erickson's often-used teaching stories, some case examples, some personal and family anecdotes, with commentary and organization by Rosen.

Walters, C. and Havens, R.A. (1993) *Hypnotherapy for Health, Harmony and Peak Performance: Expanding the Goals of Psychotherapy*. New York: Brunner/Mazel.

Yapko, M. (1986) *Hypnotic and Strategic Interventions: Principle and Practice*. New York: Irvington.

Yapko, M. (1990) *Trancework* (2nd edn). New York: Brunner/Mazel.

Yapko, M. (1992) *Hypnosis and the Treatment of Depressions: Strategies for Change*. New York: Brunner/Mazel.

Yapko, M. (1995) *Essentials of Hypnosis*. New York: Brunner/Mazel.

Zeig, J. (ed. with commentary) (1980) *A Teaching Seminar with Milton H. Erickson*. New York: Brunner/Mazel.

Transcript of a five-day teaching seminar that Erickson gave near the end of his life. It includes a number of anecdotes, some inductions and dialogues with students. Introductory chapters by Zeig on Erickson's use of anecdotes. Includes a discussion and commentary by Erickson and Zeig on a trance induction which occurred during the seminar. Spotlights Erickson's unique oral teaching ability.

Zeig, J. (ed.) (1982) *Ericksonian Approaches to Hypnosis and Psychotherapy*. New York: Brunner/Mazel.

Edited proceedings of the First International Congress on Ericksonian Approaches to Hypnosis and Psychotherapy, which was held in Phoenix, Arizona in 1980. Includes keynote addresses by Jay Haley and Carl Whitaker, and 41 papers on Erickson and Ericksonian approaches in various areas of social science and medicine.

Zeig, J. (ed.) (1985a) *Ericksonian Psychotherapy, Vol. I: Structures*. New York: Brunner/Mazel.

Zeig, J. (ed.) (1985b) *Ericksonian Psychotherapy, Vol. II: Clinical Applications*. New York: Brunner/Mazel.

These are the edited proceedings of the Second International Erickson Congress, held in Phoenix in 1983. Keynote and plenary addresses are by Watzlawick, Rossi, Haley and Madanes. Includes a special section by Erickson's family on his child-rearing techniques. These volumes are meant to show the development and furthering of Erickson's work in new directions or to show new applications for Erickson's techniques and approaches.

Zeig, J. (ed.) (1985c) *Experiencing Erickson: An Introduction to the Man and His Work*. New York: Brunner/Mazel.

This book contains an overview and introduction to Erickson as a person and as a therapist, as well as transcripts of Erickson's supervision and teaching with Zeig.

Zeig, J. (ed.) (1987) *The Evolution of Psychotherapy: The First Conference*. New York: Brunner/Mazel.

This book contains the edited proceedings of 27 presentations given at the first Evolution of Psychotherapy Conference, a landmark meeting held in Phoenix, Arizona in 1985.

Zeig, J. (ed.) (1992) *The Evolution of Psychology: The Second Conference*. New York: Brunner/Mazel.

This book contains the edited proceedings of the second Evolution Conference, which was held in Anaheim, California. It includes the presentations and question/answer sessions of 23 distinguished faculty members.

Zeig, J. (ed.) (1994) *Ericksonian Methods: The Essence of the Story*. New York: Brunner/Mazel.

Zeig, J. (ed.) (1997) *The Evolution of Psychotherapy: The Third Conference*. New York: Brunner/Mazel.

Zeig, J. and Gilligan, S. (eds) (1990) *Brief Therapy: Myths, Methods, and Metaphor*. New York: Brunner/Mazel.

This book contains the edited proceedings of the Fourth International Congress on Ericksonian Approaches to Hypnosis and Psychotherapy, held in San Francisco, California, in 1988.

Zeig, J. and Lankton, S. (eds) (1988) *Developing Ericksonian Therapy: State of the Art*. New York: Brunner/Mazel.

This book contains the edited proceedings of the Third International Congress on Ericksonian Approaches to Hypnosis and Psychotherapy, held in Phoenix, Arizona, in 1986.

Zeig, J. and Munion, W.M. (eds) (1990) *What is Psychotherapy? Contemporary Perspectives*. San Francisco: Jossey-Bass.

References

Araoz, D.L. (1985) *The New Hypnosis*. New York: Brunner/Mazel.

Bandler, R. and Grinder, J. (1975) *Patterns of the Hypnotic Techniques of Milton H. Erickson, MD. Vol. 1.* Cupertino, CA: Meta Publications.

Barber, J. (1977a) 'Rapid induction analgesia: a clinical report', *American Journal of Clinical Hypnosis*, 19 (3): 138–47.

Barber, J. (1977b) 'The efficacy of hypnotic analgesia for dental pain in individuals of both high and low hypnotic susceptibility', *Dissertation Abstracts International*, 37 (9-B): 4718.

Barber, J. (1980) 'Hypnosis and the unhypnotizable', *The American Journal of Clinical Hypnosis*, 23 (1): 4–9.

Barber, J. (1987) 'On not beating dead horses', *British Journal of Experimental and Clinical Hypnosis Special Issue: Is Hypnotherapy a Placebo?*, 4 (3): 156–7.

Barber, J. (1989) 'Suffering children hurt us', *Pediatrician*, 16 (1–2): 119–23.

Barber, J. (1993) 'The clinical role of responsivity tests: a master class commentary', *International Journal of Clinical and Experimental Hypnosis*, 41 (3): 165–8.

Barber, J. and Adrian, C. (1982) *Psychological Approaches to the Management of Pain.* New York: Brunner/Mazel.

Breggin, P.R. (1979) *Electroshock: Its Brain Disabling Effects.* New York: Springer.

Cade, B. and O'Hanlon, W.H. (1993) *A Brief Guide to Brief Therapy.* New York: Norton.

Cautela, J.R. (1993) 'Insight in behavior therapy', *Journal of Behavior Therapy and Experimental Psychiatry*, 24 (2): 93–7.

Cooper, L.E. and Erickson, M.H. (1982) *Time Distortion in Hypnosis* (2nd edn) (First published 1954). Baltimore: Williams & Wilkins.

Crasilneck, Harold B. and Hall, James A. (1975) *Clinical Hypnosis: Principles and Applications.* New York: Grune & Stratton.

de Shazer, S. (1985) *Keys to solutions in Brief Therapy.* New York: Norton.

Dolan, Y.M. (1985) *A Path with a Heart: Ericksonian Utilization with Resistant and Chronic Clients.* New York: Brunner/Mazel.

Dolan, Y.M. (1986) 'Metaphors for motivation and intervention', *Family Therapy Collections*, 19: 1–10.

Dolan, Y.M. (1989) '"Only once if I really mean it": brief treatment of a previously dissociated incest case', *Journal of Strategic and Systemic Therapies Special Issue: Childhood Sexual Abuse*, 8 (4): 3–8.

Dolan, Y.M. (1991) *Resolving Sexual Abuse: Solution-focused Therapy and Ericksonian Hypnosis for Adult Survivors.* New York: Norton.

Dolan, Y.M. (1997) 'I'll start my diet tomorrow: a solution-focused approach to weight loss', *Contemporary Family Therapy*, 19 (1): 41–8.

Edgette, J.H. and Edgette, J.S. (1995) *The Handbook of Hypnotic Phenomena in Psychotherapy*. New York: Brunner/Mazel.

Erickson, Elizabeth M. (1994) Convocation, Sixth International Congress on Ericksonian Approaches to Hypnosis and Psychotherapy. Los, Angeles, CA.

Erickson, M.H. (1932) 'Possible detrimental effects from experimental hypnosis', *Journal of Abnormal and Social Psychology*, 27: 321–7.

Erickson, M.H. (1939) 'An experimental investigation of the possible antisocial use of hypnosis', *Psychiatry*, 2: 391–414.

Erickson, M.H. (1954a) 'Special techniques of brief hypnotherapy', *Journal of Clinical and Experimental Hypnosis*, 2: 109–29.

Erickson, M.H. (1954b) 'Pseudo-orientation in time as a hypnotherapeutic procedure', *Journal of Clinical and Experimental Hypnosis*, 2: 261–83. (Also in E. Rossi [ed.] [1980d] *Collected Papers of Milton H. Erickson on Hypnosis*, Vol. IV. New York: Irvington. pp. 397–423.)

Erickson, M.H. (1958) 'Naturalistic techniques of hypnosis', *The American Journal of Clinical Hypnosis*, July (1): 3–8.

Erickson, M.H. (1959a) 'Further clinical techniques of hypnosis: utilization techniques', *The American Journal of Clinical Hypnosis*, 2 (1): 3–21.

Erickson, M.H. (1959b) 'Hypnosis in painful terminal illness', *The American Journal of Clinical Hypnosis*, 1: 117–21.

Erickson, M.H. (Circa 1960) Clinical and experimental trance: hypnotic training and time required for their development. Unpublished discussion. (Also in E. Rossi [ed.] [1980b], *The Collected Papers of Milton H. Erickson on Hypnosis*, Vol. II. New York: Irvington. pp. 301–6.)

Erickson, M.H. (1960) Expectancy and minimal sensory cues in hypnosis. Incomplete report. (Also in E. Rossi [ed.] [1980b], *The Collected Papers of Milton H. Erickson on Hypnosis*, Vol. II. New York: Irvington. pp. 337–9.)

Erickson, M.H. (1964) Initial Experiments Investigating the Nature of Hypnosis. *The American Journal of Clinical Hypnosis*, October, 7: 152–62.

Erickson, M.H. (1965a) 'The use of symptoms as an integral part of hypnotherapy', *The American Journal of Clinical Hypnosis*, 8: 57–65.

Erickson, M.H. (1965b) 'Experimental hypnotherapy in Tourette's Disease', *The American Journal of Clinical Hypnosis*, 7: 325–31.

Erickson, M.H. (1966) 'Experimental knowledge of hypnotic phenomena employed for hypnotherapy', *The American Journal of Clinical Hypnosis*, 8: 200–309.

Erickson, M.H. (1967) 'Further experimental investigation of hypnosis: hypnotic and non-hypnotic realities', *The American Journal of Clinical Hypnosis*, 10: 87–135. (Also in E. Rossi [ed.] [1980a], *The Collected Papers of Milton H. Erickson on Hypnosis*, Vol. I. New York: Irvington. pp. 18–32.)

Erickson, M.H. (1977) 'Hypnotic approaches to therapy', *The American Journal of Clinical Hypnosis*, 20 (1): 20–35.

Erickson, M.H. and Erickson, E.M. (1938) 'The hypnotic induction of halucinatory color vision followed by pseudo-negative after-images', *Journal of Experimental Psychology*, 22: 581–8.

Erickson, M.H. and Erickson, E.M. (1958) 'Further considerations of time distortion: subjective time condensation as distinct from time expansion', *The American Journal of Clinical Hypnosis*, October (1): 83–9.

Erickson, M.H., Hershman, S. and Secter, I. (1961) *The Practical Application of Medical and Dental Hypnosis*. New York: Julian Press.

Erickson, M.H. and Lustig, H.S. (1975) Verbatim transcript of the videotape, 'The Artistry of Milton H. Erickson, MD', Parts 1 and 2.

Erickson, M.H. and Rossi, E.L. (1975) 'Varieties of double bind', *The American Journal of Clinical Hypnosis*, 17: 143–57.

Erickson, M.H. and Rossi, E.L. (1979) *Hypnotherapy: An Exploratory Casebook.* New York: Irvington.

Furman, B. and Ahola, T. (1994) 'Solution talk: the solution-oriented way of talking about problems', in M. Hoyt (ed.), *Constructive Therapies*. New York: Guilford Press.

Gilligan, S.G. (1997) *The Courage to Love: Principles and Practices of Self-relations Psychotherapy*. New York: Norton.

Gilligan, S.G. (ed.) (1993) *Therapeutic Conversations*. New York: Norton.

Gilligan, S.G. and Price, R. (1987) *Therapeutic Trances: The Cooperation Principle in Ericksonian Hypnotherapy*. New York: Brunner/Mazel.

Haley, J. (1973) *Uncommon Therapy: The Psychiatric Techniques of Milton H. Erickson MD*. New York: Norton.

Haley, J. (ed.) (1985a) *Conversations with Milton H. Erickson, MD, Vol. I: Changing Individuals*. New York: Triangle (Norton).

Haley, J. (ed.) (1985b) *Conversations with Milton H. Erickson, MD, Vol. II: Changing Couples*. New York: Triangle (Norton).

Haley, J. (ed.) (1985c) *Conversations with Milton H. Erickson, MD, Vol. III: Changing Children and Families*. New York: Triangle (Norton).

Haley, J. (1993) *Jay Haley on Milton H. Erickson*. New York: Brunner/Mazel.

Hammond, D.C. (1986) 'Evidence of Erickson's effectiveness', in B. Zilbergeld, M.G. Edelstein and D.L. Araoz (eds), *Hypnosis Questions and Answers*. New York: Norton.

Kazdin, A.E. (1982) 'Symptom substitution, generalization and response covariation: implications for psychotherapy outcome', *Psychological Bulletin*, 91 (2): 349–65.

Kirsch, I., Lynn, S.J. and Rhue, J.W. (1993) 'Introduction to clinical hypnosis', in J.W. Rhue, S.J. Lynn and I. Kirsch (eds), *Handbook of Clinical Hypnosis*. Washington, DC: American Psychological Association.

Lankton, C.H. (1985) 'Elements of an Ericksonian approach', in S.R. Lankton (ed.), *Elements and Dimensions of an Ericksonian Approach*. New York: Brunner/Mazel.

Lankton, S.R. (1990) 'Ericksonian strategic therapy', in J.K. Zeig and W.M. Munion (eds), *What is Psychotherapy? Contemporary Perspectives*. San Francisco: Jossey-Bass. pp. 363–71.

Lankton, S.R. and Lankton C.H. (1983) *The Answer Within: A Clinical Framework of Ericksonian Hypnotherapy*. New York: Bruner/Mazel.

Lankton, S.R. and Lankton C.H. (1986) *Enchantment and Intervention in Family Therapy: Training in Ericksonian Approaches*. New York: Bruner/Mazel.

Lankton, S.R., Gilligan, S.G. and Zeig, J.K. (1991) *Views on Ericksonian Brief Therapy, Process and Action*. New York: Brunner/Mazel.

Madanes, Cloé (1987) 'Advances in strategic family therapy', in J.K. Zeig (ed.), *The Evolution of Psychotherapy: First Conference*. New York: Brunner/Mazel. pp. 46–55.

Mead, Margaret (1976) 'The originality of Milton Erickson', *The American Journal of Clinical Hypnosis*, 20 (1): 4–5.

O'Hanlon, W.H. (1987) *Taproots: Underlying Principles of Milton Erickson's Therapy and Hypnosis*. New York: Norton.

O'Hanlon, W.H. and Hexum, A.L. (1990) *An Uncommon Casebook: The Complete Clinical Work of Milton H. Erickson*. New York: Norton.

O'Hanlon, W.H. and Hudson, P.O. (1994) 'Coauthoring a love story: solution-oriented marital therapy', in M.F. Hoyt (ed.), *Constructive Therapies*. New York: Guilford Press.

O'Hanlon, W.H. and Martin, M. (1992) *Solution-oriented Hypnosis: An Ericksonian Approach*. New York: Norton.

O'Hanlon, W.H. and Weiner-Davis, M. (1989) *In Search of Solutions: A New Direction in Psychotherapy*. New York: Norton.

Price, D.D. and Barber, J. (1987) 'An analysis of factors that contribute to the efficacy of hypnotic analgesia', *Journal of Abnormal Psychology*, 96 (1): 46–51.

Random House Dictionary (1994) Unabridged electronic dictionary. New York: Random House.

Rosen, S. (1982) *My Voice Will Go with You: The Teaching Tales of Milton H. Erickson*. New York: Norton.

Rosen, S. (1988) 'What makes Ericksonian therapy so effective?', in J.K. Zeig and S.R. Lankton (eds), *Developing Ericksonian Therapy: State of the Art*. New York: Brunner/Mazel.

Rossi, E.L. (ed.) (1980a) *The Collected Papers of Milton H. Erickson on Hypnosis. Vol. I: The Nature of Hypnosis and Suggestion*. New York: Irvington.

Rossi, E.L. (ed.) (1980b) *The Collected Papers of Milton H. Erickson on Hypnosis. Vol. II: Hypnotic Alteration of Sensory, Perceptual and Psychophysiological Processes*. New York: Irvington.

Rossi, E.L. (ed.) (1980c) *The Collected Papers of Milton H. Erickson on Hypnosis. Vol. III: Hypnotic Investigation of Psychodynamic Processes*. New York: Irvington.

Rossi, E.L. (ed.) (1980d) *The Collected Papers of Milton H. Erickson on Hypnosis. Vol. IV: Innovative Hypnotherapy*. New York: Irvington.

Rossi, E.L. and Ryan, Margaret O. (eds) (1985) *Life Reframing in Hypnosis: The Seminars, Workshops and Lectures of Milton H. Erickson. Vol. II*. New York: Irvington.

Rossi, E.L., Ryan, Margaret O. and Sharp, Florence A. (1983) *Healing in Hypnosis: The Seminars, Workshops and Lectures of Milton H. Erickson. Vol. I*. New York: Irvington.

Weitzenhoffer, A.M. (1989) *The Practice of Hypnotism. Vol. II*. New York: John Wiley.

Yapko, M.D. (1988) *When Living Hurts: Directives for Treating Depression*. New York: Brunner/Mazel.

Yapko, M.D. (ed.) (1989) *Brief Therapy Approaches to Treating Anxiety and Depression*. New York: Brunner/Mazel.

Yapko, M.D. (1990) 'Directive psychotherapy', in J.K. Zeig and W.M. Munion (eds), *What is Psychotherapy? Contemporary Perspectives*. San Francisco: Jossey-Bass.

Yapko, M.D. (1992) *Hypnosis and the Treatment of Depressions: Strategies for Change*. New York: Brunner/Mazel.

Zeig, J.K. (1980) *A Teaching Seminar with Milton H. Erickson*. New York: Brunner/Mazel.

Zeig, J.K. (1985) *Experiencing Erickson: An Introduction to the Man and his Work*. New York: Brunner/Mazel.

Zeig, J.K. (1990a) 'Seeding', in J.K. Zeig and S. Gilligan (eds), *Brief Therapy: Myths, Methods, and Metaphors*. New York: Brunner/Mazel. pp. 221–46.

Zeig, J.K. (1990b) 'Ericksonian psychotherapy', in J.K. Zeig and W.M. Munion (eds), *What is Psychotherapy? Contemporary Perspectives*. San Francisco: Jossey-Bass.

Zeig, J.K. (1992) 'The virtues of our faults: a key concept of Ericksonian therapy', in J.K. Zeig (ed.), *The Evolution of Psychotherapy, Second Conference*. New York: Brunner/Mazel. pp. 252–66.

Zeig, J.K. and Geary, B.B. (1990) 'Seeds of strategic and interactional psychotherapies: seminal contributors of Milton H. Erickson', *The American Journal of Clinical Hypnosis*, 33: 105–12.

Zeig, J.K. and Gilligan, S.G. (eds) (1990) *Brief Therapy: Myths, Methods and Metaphors*. New York: Brunner/Mazel.

Zeig, J.K. and Munion, W.M. (eds) (1990) *What is Psychotherapy? Contemporary Perspectives*. San Francisco: Jossey-Bass.

Zilbergeld, B., Edelstein, M.G. and Araoz, D.L. (eds) (1986) *Hypnosis Questions and Answers*. New York: Norton.

Index